**NEIGHBOR
EMPLOYER
FRIEND
RELATIVE
SPOUSE**

Any one of these may be an alcoholic.
Sometimes you may know it. Sometimes you
may not.

Here is everything you never thought you'd
need to know about alcoholism . . .
    possible causes
    case histories
    statistics
    medical and psychiatric opinion
    treatment
. . . even a self-scoring RAP scale to measure
your own Risk of Addictive Problems.

**Over nine million people need help in the
United States alone.**

THE 13th AMERICAN is a sobering book. It
was meant to be.

About The Author

Pastor Paul, a long-time member of Alcoholics Anonymous, proves that alcoholism can strike in any profession. He numbers among his friends many ministers, priests and nuns who have been led out of the abyss of problem drinking through the gracious hand of a loving God——and the fellowship of A.A.

This is his story. He does not presume to speak for A.A. But he readily attributes his own recovery to this fellowship of men and women who shared their experience, strength and hope with him when he "hit bottom" and saw only insanity or death on the horizon. Today he stands in his pulpit as Exhibit A for those skeptics who would deny that human nature can be redeemed.

Pastor Paul received high honors from both his college and seminary. He also holds two masters degrees——one in public administration and international relations, and the other in pastoral care and counseling. He is presently pursuing doctoral studies at New York University.

He is a frequent speaker on alcoholism, and has written on the subject for several periodicals in the United States and abroad, including Christianity Today and The Christian Herald. He recently appeared on a special broadcast of the Lutheran Hour with Dr. Oswald Hoffmann.

Pastor Paul attended the 1965 summer school of the Rutgers Center for Alcohol Studies, and the 1972 summer sessions at the Berkeley Center for Alcohol Studies.

THE 13TH AMERICAN

PASTOR PAUL

David C. Cook Publishing Co.
850 NORTH GROVE AVENUE • ELGIN, IL 60120
In Canada: David C. Cook Publishing (Canada) Ltd., Weston, Ontario M9L 1T4

THE 13TH AMERICAN

Copyright © 1973 David C. Cook Publishing Co.

David C. Cook Publishing Co., Elgin, IL 60120

Printed in the United States of America
Library of Congress Catalog Number: 73-78711

ISBN: 0-912692-12-X

CONTENTS

5

To my beloved Myrt whose faith, hope,
and love have given me serenity in my
treasured sobriety; and to John T.,
A.A. sponsor and friend, whose exemplary
life and charming Irish blarney taught
me how to recover from alcoholism.

1

I Sat Where They Sat

"Then I came to them of the captivity of Tel-abib, that dwelt by the river of Chebar, and I sat where they sat, and remained there astonished among them seven days" (Ezekiel 3: 15 KJV).

THREE HARD YEARS of theological training were fast drawing to a close as an ominous rap on the door of our seminary apartment made me suddenly panic as I desperately slid the shot glass under the chair with my foot.

My beloved Myrt moved toward the door as I hastily attempted to further conceal the amber liquid with the nearby footstool. As she opened it, I could see the figure of the man who was responsible for my leaving journalism to enter the ministry.

His name was Dr. Jarvis M. Cotton, the seminary's vice-president, and almost a second father to my wife and me. It was Dr. Cotton who had interviewed me as a prospective student the day after I had slept off a drunk under a table in one of Cleveland's better hotels. But he knew nothing of the physical and emotional pain I was feeling that day as he paved the way for my family to get on-campus living quarters.

A sharp pain in the pit of my stomach told me that

Dr. Cotton no longer was ignorant of my serious drinking problem. I had thought that I had been able to conceal my battle with the bottle from both my professors and fellow students. But the nervous tinge to Dr. Cotton's voice told me that the jig was finally up.

"Hi," he said, "I've got something I'd like to talk over with Paul."

That "something" chilled me to the marrow as he spied the shot and a beer plainly visible beneath my chair. I thought the recital of the incriminating evidence would never end as I visualized three hard years of work going down the barroom drain.

. . . The maintenance man had blown the whistle on the number of liquor bottles found in our garbage cans.

. . . Fellow students, some not above taking a drink themselves, had expressed either concern or consternation over my drinking habits.

Painfully the last of the evidence was placed on the table. I was badly shaken, and the girl who was about to present me with our second son had been reduced to tears. It was then that Jarv Cotton's voice took on a fatherly tone.

He made it clear that no one had any desire to bar me from the ministry, that he and others had a genuine interest in my wife and me as persons. But he did want to warn me of what had happened to others who thought they could enter into a pact with John Barleycorn and still retain their reputations, sanity and health.

Now there is a widespread belief, especially among members of Alcoholics Anonymous, that only an alcoholic can help the brother or sister who still suffers. And while there is no little truth in that rubric, Jarvis Cotton did all that could be expected of any man that day he rapped on our apartment door. He showed great Christlike compassion; but he also made me face the fact that drinking could lead to disaster.

8

Dr. Cotton didn't call me an alcoholic. I think he shared my deep-seated belief that my aberrant drinking pattern had developed as a direct result of an exhausting schedule in a special honors program at the seminary. I didn't bother to tell him that I wrote a major portion of my senior thesis in a neighborhood gin mill.

My thoughts were directed, rather, to the new baby and to the prospects of being ordained and installed as the pastor of one of the nicest churches in Western Pennsylvania. "I think this problem will clear up the minute we settle down in our new church," I said.

Jarvis Cotton was satisfied. He kissed Myrt, shook hands with me, then left with the confidence that he had accomplished a job which was as painful for him as it was to me. My own shaken composure told me I needed that drink underneath the chair. I cursed its stranglehold even as I felt its warmth nurse away the pain.

Little did I know then that I was building an elaborate defense system to rationalize my need for the next drink. I was forever blaming other people or my environment for my mad rush into alcoholic oblivion.

I finished second highest in my class. But the runner-up award brought with it only extreme self-pity and resentment as I chafed in the knowledge that I was knocked from the academic pinnacle by two men who had taken an intern year away from the drudgery of classes. Only recently did I manage to get this monkey off my back.

Yet I sincerely looked for a new and easier life following installation in my first parish. I had not yet come to realize the futility of so-called geographical cures. The sway of the amber liquid made it impossible for me to see the correlation between my hopes for a sober future and my initial decision to leave the newsroom for the classroom in an effort to get away from alcohol. I should have remembered that I searched out the nearest gin mill that first night on campus, my body occupying a barstool even as I vowed to swear off booze for a lifetime.

I was still unaware of the insidious complexities of alcoholism even as my seminary education drew to a close. But already I was beginning to sense that I didn't drink like other people. I did not drink for sociability's sake, nor because I liked the taste. In fact, I hated it. I drank solely for the effect. As an A.A. oldtimer was to remark of alcohol later in my drinking career, "It's the oldest tranquilizer known to man."

My uneasy conscience led me to read a book while my wife was recuperating in the maternity wing of a nearby hospital. It was called *The Prodigal Shepherd,* and it told the candid story of a Roman Catholic priest who recovered from alcoholism after almost being drummed out of the priesthood. I devoured every word until my eyelids closed under the influence of the wine that rested on the table next to the bed.

A funny thing began to happen about that time. I noticed that I might stay away from booze for a week or two, as I wrestled with current problems in light of the evangelical faith of my childhood. But as soon as I picked up a drink, I could not stop. One drink invariably led to a drunk. I could change drinks, or devise any number of elaborate schemes; but once I picked up that first drink, one was too many and a thousand were not enough!

Even the thrill of moving into our first manse was dwarfed by the rat race of making sure that I knew where to get the next drink. My wife and I genuinely loved the flock entrusted to our care. They were wonderful people, and no request was too great—if it would make the young minister and his wife happy. They shamefully spoiled us in their attempt to make us feel at home.

At the outset, the congregation responded to my warmly evangelical preaching. For even in my blackest moments I found it impossible to depart from the faith "once delivered unto the saints." But this very fact led me into deeper despair, as the depth of my own hypocrisy seared my soul. My only relief came from another round of drinks. And soon a bottle rested on the desk as I agonized over next Sunday's sermon—a sermon that would undoubtedly reflect my theological convictions but would be devoid of any conviction at the feeling level. I was a fake!

But the worst moments came as I made an extremely limited number of parish and hospital calls. For about this time I discovered that my nerves and the growing tremors in my hands could be brought under control by taking a few fast nips. I knew that a drink or two would do the trick; but I could never stop there. Either I would drink until I fell asleep, or I would face the fierce anxiety that my breath, my bearing, or my speech would betray my weakness as I was forced to go out into the public.

I knew that I could not risk being seen in gin mills, although the pain was sometimes so great that I would occasionally duck into one with the prayer that no one would see me. More often, I would stop at a state liquor store while making a hospital call in a neighboring community. I would load up with a couple gallon jugs of cheap wine—enough to last me until my next visit.

However, I often failed to reckon with my increasing tolerance for alcohol. Whereas a few drinks would give me that mellow feeling in the early years, I now required much more in order to get the glow. Consequently, I often ran short of my most treasured possession. I would therefore wait until the congregation was safely tucked into bed at night, and then I would steal out to a nearby tavern—there to occupy a barstool until the bartender hollered in the dawn's early light, "Last call for alcohol!"

Summer time is always best for an alcoholic because the gin mills are generally permitted to remain open that extra hour for Daylight Savings Time. One of the worst days is election day when most states forbid the sale of alcoholic beverages while the polls are open. On the other hand, any alcoholic worth his cherries and olives— or in the condition to do so—always hibernates with his hidden supply when the electoral process interferes with his favorite sport.

My problem wasn't booze. It was work. It was other people. It was money. All of them limited my ability to do the thing that mattered most in life. And that was to drink. I literally drank to live. And I lived to drink. Any other pursuit was secondary by this time.

Something had to give. I suddenly realized the full meaning of Dr. Cotton's warning that an alcoholic so often pulls his family down along with himself. I knew in my heart that I would bring scandal upon my family and upon Christ and His Church if I didn't stop drinking immediately and completely. Yet I was powerless to do so.

There is a saying among alcoholics that God takes care of drunks and little boys. He certainly was looking out for me. What's more, while my congregation didn't realize it at the time, God was also looking out for His flock in that Western Pennsylvania community.

What happened next demands a bit of explanation. In my last two years as a newsman, I had covered some of the major religious gatherings at Buck Hill Falls in Pennsylvania—the Episcopal House of Bishops, the various denominational agencies, and the World and National Councils of Churches. In the process, I had made friends with some of the top reporters covering the religion beat, as well as many top denominational and conciliar officials. But none of them were aware of my serious drinking problem.

Yet the telephone call I received early one morning strained even my credulity. The voice on the other end was that of one of America's most distinguished church-men. When I finally hung up, I rushed upstairs to tell my wife the good news.

"They want us to go to Europe," I said, "to begin press relations for a big meeting in Asia next year."

A sleepy spouse told me to check the telephone again —and then let her in on the real message.

But it was no joke. It was for real. And shortly there-after I had a telegram from Europe to prove it. The very words "Invite you to join the staff of . . ." held out the promise of one great big geographical cure.

It wasn't too difficult to rationalize why we should leave a congregation which had welcomed us into its heart only a few months before. I was able to argue that people were already cooling toward us . . . that this was a chance of a lifetime that would prove to my members that they really didn't appreciate what a wonderful min-ister they had.

They *were* lucky people. Lucky, that is, that they were going to see me leave before I caused heartache to my family and scandal in this lovely community.

For now every effort and emotion called for another drink. I badly neeeded a few martinis to quiet my nerves after the bumpy DC-3 flight from Pennsylvania to New York. And I certainly needed an ample liquid send-off as we bid adieu to family and friends at the gangplank of the Queen Elizabeth. As we pulled out of our berth and past the Statue of Liberty, I silently promised that things would be different abroad.

But they were not. In fact, the very first words I learned in French were *Encore un, s'il vous plait*. My life depended upon them. Roughly translated they meant, "Can I have another drink, please?"

Europe turned out to be an alcoholic's paradise. Gone were the social taboos of America. Wine was as readily available as milk on the supermarket shelves. Policemen felt no censure if they dropped into a cafe for *un carafe* of *vin ordinaire* while taking a break from traffic duty. I could walk into the Cafe du Union and order a beer and rotgut cognac for about 30 cents. And, while martinis were unavailable except in places catering to rich American tourists, I quickly learned that I could ask for Cinzano *avec* gin. How often I literally prayed that there would be just a dash of vermouth and an extra amount of gin!

However, any alcoholic should think twice before hopping the next plane to French-speaking Europe. For my knowledge of bistros offering the cheapest *vin et alcool* involved a matter of life and death. Only bitter memories remain of those days when my then 10-year-old son manfully tried to open wine and whiskey bottles for a father who was shaking so badly that he thought he would jump right out of his skin. My beloved wife had come to the point where she herself thought that my booze was more important than food for the family. It certainly is anything but comforting to remember the day that I threw out the horse meat my wife had bought with an empty pocketbook in a last-ditch effort to keep body and soul together. Even in our poverty, my alcoholic megalomania demanded that I retain the air of one of the last of the bigtime spenders. But each morning I had to face the real me. And I couldn't face myself in the mirror—unless my ego was bolstered by a couple of early morning belts.

Christians so often ask how a minister of the Gospel could possibly "sink so low"—a rhetorical question generally answered in light of their own theological perspective. Others who have lacked my educational and vocational advantages may excuse their own drinking but condemn me for "blowing it" when I "had it made." Still others wonder aloud why my wife didn't get rid of the bum. She certainly had the opportunity—since a sober and sainted seminary professor once invited her to go to

14

bed with someone other than a drunken husband.

Now I certainly would be the last to defend my alcoholic behavior. However, those who view alcoholism in purely moralistic terms might consider the agony from which I was unable to extricate either myself or my family. I lived in daily panic that I would lose my job and leave my wife and two sons stranded in Europe. And, although a strong wind could blow me over at the time, I had developed a tolerance for two litres of wine and a fifth of gin a day. That's not counting the nips I downed to and from work and at afternoon tea time. Surely a sophisticated sinner would not put himself through such agony. He'd have better sense.

There were times as I rode the tram to work that I passed a building that had written on one of its exterior walls *Hopital pour Alcoolisme*. I often wondered if they could do anything for me. My stomach was shot. My nerves danced a macabre dance in Dante's "Inferno." And, while I was ignorant of the disease called alcoholism at the time, I was just beginning to associate some of my physical symptoms with my unusual drinking habits.

But it was not until my family and I returned to the United States that I was really able to put two and two together. I had taken a new public relations post with a major Protestant denomination just a few days after my arrival in good old America. My first assignment was in Atlantic City, and I can remember sweating and shaking through the endless round of sessions, unable to eat and barely able to lift a cup of coffee without spilling the contents all over the table. Then, in rapid succession, came Chicago, Sacramento, and a host of other strange and lonely cities across the country. I didn't take any pictures. But I sure had a lot to drink. I was on a perpetual merry-go-round. And I couldn't catch the brass ring.

My beloved wife dreaded the dawn of each new day. For it meant that she would have to answer the bill collectors, or cringe when opening another dunning letter or telegram. You certainly can't pay bills and buy alcohol at the same time. It was a simple matter of priorities. And booze came before $2,000 in long-overdue debts.

But God was standing in the shadows keeping watch over one of His own, lost though he was in the far country. For we had moved to West New York, New Jersey, upon our return to the United States. Little did we know at the time that help literally waited around the corner.

It was a Saturday night. The children were both in bed. My wife was sitting on the living room couch, while I nursed an almost-full bottle of wine. We both were sick at heart. I knew that life was meant to offer much more than this. And even in my alcoholic loneliness and isolation, I knew that I still loved my wife and that she still loved the man she had originally married. Suddenly I found myself kneeling by her beside the couch, and I began to cry, "Honey, I'll do anything. Anything!"

"Can I call A.A.?" she quietly asked.

I guess we both shared that kind of amorphous knowledge of the general public that A.A. does something for problem drinkers. Maybe the guys who end up on skid row. My only memories of A.A. involved the son of one of my former publishers who, so newsroom gossip had it, would get up at three o'clock in the morning and go out to help some drunk. But I also remembered covering a state A.A. convention as a young reporter. The keynote speaker, a well-dressed and articulate man who remained anonymous, ended his talk by saying: "The Bible says, 'Ye must be born again.' So I guess that is what happened to me."

"Sure, honey," I said. "Call A.A."

Myrt dialed Alcoholics Anonymous Intergroup, the clearinghouse for calls in the New York metropolitan area. "Gee, that's too bad," said the girl at the other end of the line. "There was a West New York meeting to-night. But maybe if you hang right up, you'll still be able to get them." She did, and so began a new phase in my alcoholic odyssey.

My bride had distinct misgivings the moment she made contact with the church in which the West New York group held its biweekly meetings. The gruff voice was anything but reassuring, and the boistrous laughter in the background made her certain that she had either dialed a barroom or that A.A. was a *real* drinking man's program! "Are you calling for yourself or someone else?" the man inquired.

"My husband," replied my still uncertain Myrt.

"Well put him on the line."

Slowly, and with unsteady pace, I made my way to the telephone. "Hello," I mumbled.

There was something in that man's voice that told me he knew the score. He seemed to be the combination be-tween one of the bartenders I had come to know so well and a compassionate father confessor. He asked a few questions, then inquired: "Do you think you can stay away from the stuff until I get around to see you to-morrow afternoon?"

Thankful that I could at last get him off the line, I as-sured him that I could. Then I hung up and promptly went back to nurse my bottle of wine. I was lying on my bed in a drunken stupor when the doorbell rang the fol-lowing afternoon.

"Hello, my name is John," the caller said when Myrt answered the door.

"You're from A.A.?" she asked in shocked disbelief.

"What did you expect? A Bowery bum?"

Silver hair set off the ruddy Irish face. He was hand-some and impeccably attired. He was also to teach me more about Christlike living and true Christian unity than I ever learned in seminary or in the councils of churches. No man outside our family circle would ever mean more to me than John T. He was to be my A.A. sponsor. And I was to be his pigeon.

"Can I please come in?" he finally asked in exasperation.

I don't remember much about that initial meeting. Myrt tells me that I would shake my head affirmatively as John outlined his own drinking history. His experience had been my own. I could identify at every point in the downward path into alcoholism. But John didn't preach. Nor did he even faintly hint that I was an alcoholic. That was something I would have to determine for myself. All he asked at length was, "Do you think you might have a problem?"

I was filled with unbearable guilt and remorse for all the bad things I had done to my family. I felt a sharp stab of pain as I recalled parting with two crisp dollar bills given to me by a beloved rabbi friend. I had meant to spend them in Israel, but the absolute need for a drink made me part with them in a gin mill on one of my cross-country jaunts. That was also the time I somehow managed to hang on to one thin dime to call my secretary in Manhattan to ask her to call my wife in New Jersey to pick me up at John F. Kennedy Airport on Long Island. I simply had no other alternative but to beg my wife to make the long bus ride into the city with a year-old baby so that I would not have to make the long walk home. I was dead broke. But I soon regained my spirits after bumming enough money from my beloved Myrt to buy two or three martinis before daring to face the ride back home.

Did I have a problem? If John had then and there said that I was an alcoholic, I would have been greatly relieved. I thought I was either nuts or the world's greatest sinner. To be diagnosed an alcoholic would have brought sweet comfort to a man who violently shook, felt hot and cold at the same time, and often thought he would never live long enough to complete the long walk to the subway many mornings.

John was carefully looking over the 100-pound mess that sat and slobbered before him. If a man or woman can get sober cold turkey, so much the better. But some alcoholics can die from the delirium tremens or convulsions which sometimes accompany the withdrawal syndrome. The fact is, the number of fatalities resulting from medically unassisted alcohol withdrawal is even higher than that relating to heroin and other hardcore drugs. Alcoholism can be—and often is—a fatal disease. In my case, one look at me told John that I was in need of immediate hospitalization.

But Myrt and I were $2,000 in debt, and hospitals cost money. I could have probably received treatment under the major medical provisions of my denominational pension plan, although such a possibility failed to occur to me in my alcoholic fog. Knowing what I know today, I would have probably turned down such aid anyway—not because I was too proud to accept it, but because I now know of two colleagues who used sizable amounts from their pension credits to undergo analytically-oriented therapy in a country club setting. They may have learned a great deal about their own Oedipal strivings; but they failed to experience the redemptive power of Christ in their lives. Consequently, they headed for the nearest cocktail lounge the moment they were permitted to return home on a weekend pass. Neither remains in the Gospel ministry today.

Some hospitalization plans now recognize alcoholism as a legitimate disease and pay benefits accordingly. However, a conspiracy often exists within the medical profession to call the illness by anything but its proper name. It may be listed on hospital records as colitis, extreme hypertension, or as nervous exhaustion. This does a great disservice to the alcoholic because it fails to make him face his *real* problem. In my case, I couldn't have paid the price to even learn that I was suffering from a rare disease associated with eating too many lollipops. Myrt and I were dead broke!

But then something occurred which I can only explain in terms of the miracle of grace. John was a devout Irish Catholic professional man, who, from the world's standpoint, should have felt only scorn for the prodigal shepherd who had brought the Bowery into his own home. But he didn't. The priests and Levites of the Protestant community may have passed me by on the other side; but this Good Samaritan from another Christian tradition stooped down to bind my wounds and provide the money for my recovery. His compassion was born out of his gratitude to God for divine deliverance from this same Slough of Despond many years earlier.

"You know, it's a funny thing," he said slowly. "I just collected an insurance premium for my dopey uncle. It would just cover you, if you want me to take you to Mount Carmel Hospital. You can pay me back at any time."

John still kids me about that ride to Mount Carmel. "You kept saying," he recalls, " 'What is a Protestant minister doing in a car with a dopey Catholic?' " While I am sure that account is the creation of charming Irish blarney, it points up the fact that I still visualized the Church of Rome in terms of the apostate church of the Apocalypse. My A.A. contacts with priests, nuns and Catholic laymen have thankfully demolished that myth. I have found that many of them have a deeper experience of Christ in their new lives than many others who can argue long and loud on "the whole counsel of God," yet fail to keep the commandment to love one another.

Nowhere was this fact more evident than in the ministry of Mount Carmel Hospital itself. This Roman Catholic alcoholism center opened its doors in April, 1954, in a somewhat down-at-the-heels building at 396 Straight Street in Paterson, New Jersey. It was on the street called Straight that another Paul found hope to overcome the blind fury of his addiction.

This successful five-day, A.A.-oriented detoxification program is now headed by the Rev. Charles F. Grieco, who became director in 1969 at the untimely death of Monsignor William N. Wall, a gruff, middle-aged priest whose uniform was generally a baseball cap, T-shirt and faded chinos. Father Wall lived by the motto of under-standing—but not sympathy—for the alcoholic. He insisted that problem drinkers face reality, maybe for the first time in their lives. That included getting them back to the environment from which they came as soon as possible, rather than allowing them to bask in their immaturity in a country club setting. Some psychiatrists may argue that such a program fails to deal with underlying causes; but few of them can point to Mount Carmel's stunning rate of recovery. By 1970, more than 17,500 destitute and more affluent alcoholic men and women had passed through its doors. Many return at regular intervals—to carry the message of their own strength and hope to the alcoholic who still suffers.

When John and a little red-haired Irish nurse ushered me into my room, John promised me that in just a few minutes I'd "be sleeping like a baby." How right he was! I could feel the sharp jab of a needle as the drug was administered to ward off serious withdrawal complications. I didn't awaken until the next morning when I walked with uncertain steps into a brightly lit room of other men, and guardedly asked, "Where am I?"

I was in the famous Duffy's Tavern. I sat down in the nearest chair as a big, jovial Polish fellow approached me with a teeth-baring grin.

"Hey, kid," he said. "I'm the mayor. You don't look so

good. Let me get you a cup of coffee."

My hands shook beyond control. So the big guy gently lifted the cup to my lips and fed me like a baby. Did that hot, sweet coffee taste good! I was painfully dehydrated, and I hadn't eaten for about two weeks. Who needs to eat when you need a drink bad enough? But right now I treasured every sip of the warm beverage— that divine brew whose healing properties I would enjoy by the gallon at hundreds of A.A. meetings the world over in years to come. You don't have to like coffee to join A.A. but it helps!

However, right now my attention was diverted by a terribly ill Puerto Rican boy in a wheelchair trying manfully to push his way into our midst. He had been brought into Mount Carmel about the same time as I. But he was even more washed out. He had been drinking "King Kong," a powerful, if not deadly, kind of bootleg booze known in every ghetto and barrio throughout the country. He was the only man I was ever to meet who claimed that he had drunk alcohol after taking Antabuse without suffering any serious side effects.

My new Polish friend had ended up at Mount Carmel after enjoying a long period of sobriety in Alcoholics Anonymous. He had gotten overconfident and had forgotten that beer can be just as poisonous to the alcoholic as the so-called "hard stuff." He had rationalized himself into a drunk. He was on vacation. His wife was away. And he thought there would be no harm in sitting out in his backyard with a nice cold six-pack. But the beer didn't give him the desired jolt. So he thought he'd try "just one" shot of "something better." His defenses and inhibitions lost in the warm glow, he kept right on drinking himself into a bed at Mount Carmel.

Then there was the middle-aged man who sat in lonely isolation and dejection, oblivious to the lively banter around him. He was a corporate lawyer, and he had been admitted at the request of his company's enlightened medical department. He not only worried about whether a job awaited him upon his discharge; but he was equally upset about the apartment he had left in a shambles during a drunken rage.

All of us were so different—a clergyman, a lawyer, a construction worker, and an unemployed Spanish-speaking boy. We came from different backgrounds. We had different drinking patterns. Alcoholics Anonymous would have called the lawyer and me "high bottom drunks," while the lad on "King Kong" would come to refer to himself as a "low bottom drunk." Yet all of us were brothers under the skin. None of us had ended up on the Bowery. Worse yet, we had brought the Bowery into our homes. It didn't matter what we drank or how much we drank. All that mattered is what drink did to us!

The regimen at Mount Carmel was just what the doctor ordered. Up early in the morning. A good nourishing breakfast. Then our "martinis" (a tranquilizing drug administered in decreasing doses) and a healthy shot of vitamin B complex. Hospital regulations demanded that we could not retire to our beds during the day. This rule had the twin benefits of getting us back on a regular schedule and forcing us out of our alcoholic isolation and into long hours of A.A. shoptalk. Meetings were held at night, and often an individual A.A. member would drop in to check up on his "pigeon." Lights-out came after our bedtime "martinis" and a late evening snack from the well-filled refrigerator.

Mount Carmel does not claim to be "sponsored" by Alcoholics Anonymous because A.A., while eternally grateful for such services, "is not allied with any sect, denomination, politics, organization or institution." It "neither endorses nor opposes any causes." Its single-minded "purpose is to stay sober and help other alcoholics to achieve sobriety."

Therefore, John's evening visits literally did as much for him as they meant to me. Even though I had badly neglected my wife and family, the fear of losing my loved ones and my job increased as sobriety began to become more than an impossible possibility. As John sat there with me, he brought me hope that all was not lost. And the badly shaken figure of a man haunted by guilt, fear and remorse helped to keep his "memory green."

Duffy's Tavern was our day room. The ubiquitous coffeepot lay on a bar like a chalice. The well-stocked refrigerator provided soft drinks and snacks between meals. A friendly Irish setter would sometimes amble in to remind us of some of life's normal enjoyments which had for so long been lost in an alcoholic haze. The dog seemed to assure us that God was still in His Heaven and that all was right with the world.

By the time I hit Mount Carmel, I had scored a few minor personal accomplishments. I had received two high awards in journalism, gotten through college and seminary with honors, and was well-known in public relations circles in the United States and abroad. However, no recognition had ever brought the joy which I experienced that day when my big Polish friend walked over to me to inform me that he was going home. "The boys and I just took a vote," he said. "And we want you to become the new mayor of Duffy's Tavern."

Since my own discharge was but two days away, I imagine that my tenure represented the shortest mayoral administration in American history. But I can tell you that no one ever served with greater commitment and contented abandonment, counting the money in the kitty and ordering the daily provisions for our larder. The funny thing about it was that no one asked me if I was a Democrat or Republican. I was a drunk. And that was enough.

Then toward the end of my stay we were called together to meet Dr. David I. Canavan, Mount Carmel's medical director. He didn't try to explain our disease in psychoanalytical terms or attempt to drive us all back to the "primal scream." He simply laid the cold, hard facts right on the line. "You have three choices," he warned. "You can stop drinking. You can go insane. Or you can die." Such hardnosed "reality therapy" may not have touched any underlying causes. But all of us were a little quieter at the lunch table that day.

Finally, the great gettin' up morning arrived. "John is going to bring the clothes you wanted," the nurse told me privately. "He'll pick you up about eleven. But Monsignor Wall wants to see you before you go."

Panic set in at the breakfast table. John had repeatedly assured me that all was well at home. But silently I wondered. He also informed me that my boss had told Myrt that my job was waiting for me—that he sometimes wondered if he himself might have a drinking problem. The tension was only momentarily relieved when I went in for my last vitamin B shot. As I assumed the somewhat embarrassing position, I whipped out the toy hypodermic syringe which John had smuggled in the night before. I aimed it right at that cute Irish nurse, who seemed to find almost sadistic satisfaction in seeing us all jump as the needle found its mark. The boys laughed. One nurse tried to hide a faint smile.

I was still in my PJs and loose-fitting robe when I went in to see Monsignor Wall. Though attendance at mass was absolutely voluntary, I had been the monsignor's most faithful pew holder for the last five days. I remember all of the thoughts which raced through my head as I occupied a seat that first morning. "A lot of good Baptists should see me now," I mused. "Maybe they *would* like to convert me. But I'm in no position to discuss the finer points of theology right now." With that I settled back to receive God's blessing of the morning.

"I didn't want to see you until now," Father Wall said at length. "I never see any of the priests or ministers while they're undergoing treatment. That might interfere with their relationship with the other fellows."

The monsignor echoed the same warning given to me by Jarvis Cotton a few years earlier. He told me of the priests he had known whose ministries were completely ruined by alcohol. I was completely disarmed by the man's warmth and integrity as he bid me good-bye and wished me well in the future. Unhappily, Father Wall lost his own life in a tractor accident in 1969.

As I left his office, the nurse told me that John had just arrived with my black clerical suit. I had decided not to wear the collar. But it still felt good to shed the baggy PJs and robe and get dressed in the clothes of a sober man. I felt an undying sense of gratitude to God and to my Roman Catholic brethren—who had given me a new lease on life when all my Protestant friends could offer was soup and dried bread from a rescue mission kitchen.

Then I walked back into Duffy's Tavern for the last time. I shook hands all around and dropped two one dollar bills in the kitty. The little Peurto Rican lad looked at me with astonishment, and remarked: "Gee. You look like a preacher."

He was still trying to get at the truth of the matter as I jumped into John's new Olds and headed into the sunlight and home.

2

Lonely Is the Rebel

". . . my new life tells me to do right, but the old nature that is still inside me loves to sin. Oh, what a terrible predicament I'm in! Who will free me from my slavery to this deadly lower nature? Thank God! It has been done by Jesus Christ our Lord. He has set me free" (Romans 7: 23-25 LB).

JOHN HAD STOPPED OFF at our apartment following my admission into Mount Carmel to let Myrt know a little more about the place and to introduce her to A.A.'s program for recovery. He also revealed he had to stop at a gin mill on the way to the hospital so that I could fortify myself for the ordeal which lay ahead. He sipped a coke while I downed three or four quick boilermakers.

"You mean to say," she asked in shocked disbelief, "you *let* him drink?"

John knew only too well that no one can stop the alcoholic from doing anything. He'll always find a drink if he's hurting badly enough. Tears and threats avail nothing. But John also knew Myrt wasn't interested in long, drawn-out explanations at that time. "What are you worried about," he growled. "He was only kissing the stuff good-bye."

One would have thought my Mount Carmel experience would have taught me a lesson for a lifetime. But such was not the case. John's optimism and Myrt's prayers were not to be rewarded for years to come.

Not that I didn't love the A.A. way of life. I fell in love with the program the first night John picked us up to attend our first open meeting of the West New York group. Myrt was as excited as I as we made our way down into the smoke-filled basement of Trinity Reformed Church. The rich aroma of fresh coffee was only muted by the laughter of an unusually large number of happy and well-dressed men and women. All of them were sober.

"Come on," John beckoned. "I want to introduce you to a few people."

Myrt entered into the lively spirit of the meeting immediately. It was the first time she had been to a social event in many months. For a few brief moments, she could laugh and forget about the pile of bills that rested on the dining room table.

I found the introductions extremely painful. It was only because John was standing there as a strong right arm that I didn't turn tail and run. I was so unsure of myself. I felt as if a hundred X ray eyes were penetrating the phony that stood before them. It was the first time in years I had attended a social event without first being bolstered by a few stiff drinks. I sure needed one then.

But John quickly introduced me to a cherubic little fellow named Fred. He had almost been cashiered out of the Armed Forces because of his love for the sauce. He was laughing so hard that tears streamed down his face as he recounted how he was severely reprimanded during World War II for filling the shell racks in his tank with bottles requisitioned from a French wine cellar. "They fit so beautifully," he said with a trace of nostalgia.

I sipped "the best coffee in A.A." as John buttonholed

a thin, gray-haired Irishman. "Joe," he said, "I want you to meet Paul and Myrt."

There was obvious pain in Joe's face as he held out his hand. He was an "old timer" in A.A. with seventeen years of sobriety. But then something happened. After all of those years, he had a "slip," and had been discharged from Mourt Carmel only a couple of weeks before I was. That night he was a beginner all over again, facing many men he had "twelve stepped" in years past. How did he have the courage to make a comeback? "Where else do we drunks have a place to go?" he replied.

Joe's brush with near disaster had started innocently enough. His son had just been graduated from the U.S. Naval Academy at Annapolis. He and his wife had gone for the festivities. And for one split second, Joe forgot he was an alcoholic. He picked up a drink and in no time he was back where he left off seventeen years earlier.

There was a rap of the gavel at the speaker's table as the attractive crowd carried coffee and ashtrays to empty seats. "Good evening, ladies and gentlemen," said the chairman. "Welcome to the Saturday night open meeting of the West New York Group of Alcoholics Anonymous. My name is Frank and I am an alcoholic. If you're new tonight, just sit back, relax and listen. And stick around for coffee and cake after the meeting. That's when we have some of the best A.A."

I simply can't remember a single word either of the speakers said that night. But I had already learned many lessons which were to stand me in good stead in years to come. I had always thought it just wasn't possible to "have fun" without alcohol. Yet here was Fred and a host of other happy people who could laugh again. They could even see the humor in past episodes which had once caused them pain. None of them fit the stereotype of the skid row derelict. There were housewives, secretaries, a couple of grandmothers, and an assortment of policemen, clergymen, lawyers, accountants, construction workers, and a sandhog. All were well-heeled, and the line of new cars outside of the church gave lie to the expression that "A.A. can't promise you anything but your sobriety."

I had also learned an important lesson from Joe. He was the first to provide tangible evidence that alcoholism is a progressive disease. For a reason known only to God, any man or woman who has crossed that invisible line from social to alcoholic drinking can never safely imbibe again. Once an alcoholic always an alcoholic. A man may recover from alcoholism; but he can never be cured. The disease seems to continue its course even during long years of sobriety. Both Joe and my beer-drinking Polish friend discovered to their sorrow that one drink inevitably leads to a drunk.

Myrt and I went home that night grateful to God for the new life that waited in the wings.

The A.A. program seemed so simple. No one asked you to sign a pledge. All that was required for A.A. membership was the desire to stop drinking. They called it the Twenty-Four Hour Program, and immediately my thoughts went back to the words of our Lord: "Be not anxious for your life, what ye shall eat, *or what ye shall drink* . . . For tomorrow will be anxious for the things of itself. Sufficient unto the day is the evil thereof" (Matthew 6: 25, 34).

The A.A. program may have been *simple;* but it wasn't *easy.* The trick was, they told me, to stay away from one drink one day at a time. That may sound like a lark to the nondrinker or the social drinker; but for the alcoholic this rubric involved superhuman effort. Its mastery could only be attained by sticking close to others within the A.A. fellowship. "Meetings are our medicine," I was told. "Try to make ninety meetings in ninety days.

Then the door swings both ways. You can remain in the program, or you can go out and have a real blast with all of the money you saved during three months of sobriety."

Some new members were not fortunate enough to be freed from the physical compulsion at a place like Mount Carmel. Those who tried to make the program cold turkey often had to divide the first three or four twenty-four hours into more manageable time units, during which they resolved not to pick up that first drink. Sober alcoholics who had gone the route before them would often sit by their side, helping them to resist the terrifying urge for the next 15 minutes, as their bodies cried out for alcohol by shaking violently and breaking out into hot and cold sweats. Yet somehow the first twenty-four hours passed . . . and the next . . . and the next. Gradually the craving abated, and the new A.A. member began to feel like his old self, as he wolfed down coffee and his first nourishment in many days.

But A.A. told us that alcoholism is a three-fold disease—mental, physical and spiritual. The mere absence of alcohol in the body does not assure continued sobriety. Basic personality patterns have to be changed. The alcoholic is something like Pavlog's dog. He is guided by a strong stimulus-response mechanism which tells him when to pick up a drink. If he has a fight with his wife or boss, that calls for a drink. If he just won a promotion or becomes a new father, that is also an occasion for a liquid libation. "Alcoholics Anonymous is a selfish program," I was warned. "We don't stop drinking for our wives or the boss. We do it for ourselves."

That notion bothered me no end. At this stage, I desperately wanted sobriety—but only to make amends to my family and to be productive on the job. Yet a sage commentary on the wisdom of this rubric came one night when a member explained that he would not attend a meeting because he felt like staying home to watch television. "You wouldn't even have a tv set," his sponsor growled, "if it wasn't for A.A."

That sponsor knew the road to an alcoholic hell is paved with the best of intentions. He could possibly picture many men and women who yearned to return to the so-called normal things of life at the expense of remaining active in the program, perhaps an evening before the boob tube. The football game is interrupted by a beer commercial, and slowly the salivary glands begin to beckon for the long-forgotten can of beer in the refrigerator. Or the wife switches the channel to tune in "All in the Family," and some "stinkin' think in'" begins to surface as the alcoholic explodes, "You don't appreciate me even when I'm sober. So, okay. I'll show you. I'll watch the game with the boys at the bar."

There are a few sadistic or abysmally ignorant people who might try to push a drink on an alcoholic. The sadistic are often motivated by jealousy or other problems of their own when they thrust a beer or cocktail before a man who has just tasted sobriety. "All you need is willpower," they say with a knowing air. But behind the pleasant exterior there lurks the dark hint that the alcoholic is decidedly less than a man. This message is not lost on the man who is just now beginning to regain his self-respect and sense of self-esteem.

There may be less guile behind the motives of the abysmally ignorant. They may want to show genuine hospitality or guard the alcoholic from feeling "queer." "Come on," they say, as the tray passes a man just raised from the pit of hell. "One little drink won't hurt you." What they don't realize is that one drink sooner or later always leads to a drunk. The alcoholic has lost control. And, while he may struggle to "drink like other people" for a few days or even a month, his misplaced confidence will ultimately lead him back to alcoholic guilt, remorse and despair.

However, the alcoholic's greatest enemy is the enemy within. Psychologists say that he is painfully immature, dependent, and impulsive. He also demonstrates a low threshold for pain and frustration. While others may show these same characteristics, the alcoholic turns to booze to alleviate his psychic pain. He may remain on a "dry drunk," medically sober but anything but emotionally serene. His only recourse to the inevitable "slip" is to stay close to the program, gaining insights from the experience, strength, and hope of others who really understand his problems.

Alcoholics Anonymous will tell you that a "slip" is always planned. It doesn't just happen. Some members fail to "keep their memories green" as they are restored to a semblance of normalcy and gradually drift away from the A.A. fellowship. Others subconsciously make elaborate plans for their next drunk even as they assure both wife and boss that they intend to "stay on the wagon." I myself can recall the day I defensively promised Myrt the cork would remain in the bottle as I headed off on one of my numerous public relations jaunts. And I was still reciting that pledge silently to myself as my feet moved with single-minded determination toward United Airline's 100,000 Mile Club where I could pick up a drink.

Nowhere is the irony of alcoholism more evident than in the little things which most people take for granted. Some psychologists have investigated the cause of the disease in terms of a learning experience. They will work toward a kind of behavior modification by helping the alcoholic trade his destructive behavioral patterns for more constructive ones. But still the alcoholic must face such gigantic problems as where he will relieve himself while away from home. Most people would head for a restaurant, hotel or bus terminal. But the alcoholic can only think of a gin mill. And, after all, you wouldn't use a man's john without buying a drink—and maybe even a round for the boys at the bar!

Alcoholics Anonymous' program for recovery is centered in its Twelve Steps—a plan which, with appropriate modifications, can be used by anybody for a richer, fuller life of serenity and service. Some sponsors encourage a new pigeon to take the steps "cafeteria style," taking what he wants today and leaving the rest for tomorrow. There may be some wisdom in that approach for the newcomer, particularly if he can't swallow "that God stuff." But I am an A.A. traditionalist who believes that every step represents a brilliant facet in shaping the diamond of recovery.

Most newcomers are so strung out by the time they hit A.A. that they don't have any trouble accepting the first step: "We admitted we were powerless over alcohol—that our lives had become unmanageable." The trouble comes not from an intellectual *assent* to this step but from an emotional inability to *apply* it in daily living. One A.A. gal wrote in *The Grapevine* following a "slip," that she never lost sight of the fact that she was powerless over alcohol; but she had forgotten that her life had become unmanageable. The normal problems of everyday living don't fade away in the heady aura of new-found sobriety. There are those painful times in everyone's life when he can only utter the words of A.A.'s *Serenity Prayer*: "God grant me the serenity to accept the things I cannot change, courage to change the things I can, and wisdom to know the difference."

But the first step incorporates some basic theological and psychological insights. For example, the widespread myth has it that the alcoholic could stop drinking if he only showed some willpower. The opposite comes closer to the truth. The alcoholic has too much willpower. Heaven and earth will not stop him from getting his next drink if he thinks he needs one badly enough. His wife

34

might threaten to leave him. His boss may tell him he is at the end of his rope. Preachers may paint visions of a drunkard's hell. But still he keeps on searching for alcohol. I even knew of one man who spent time in prison on a burglary rap because he broke into a tavern after the bars had closed for the night. He didn't take any money. He was simply sitting at the bar merrily slopping down the sauce when the cops came to arrest him. This man had *real* willpower!

My own drinking career was studded with superhuman willpower. I can remember that day when my boss sent me to Des Moines, Iowa, a state that outlawed liquor by the drink at that time. "I guess we won't have to worry about you this time," he said, as I picked up my flight bag and his words as a sacred challenge. I registered at the Hotel Savory upon my arrival, then went around the corner to register at a bottle club. Ten minutes after hitting Des Moines I was chuckling over my ingenuity as I nursed a drink from a bottle with my name on it.

My fears of being caught with a short supply proved equally groundless when I hit Hattiesburg, Mississippi. I had heard that Ole Miss was a "dry" state; but I had also heard rumors that bootleggers were a dime a dozen. The latter proved all-too-correct, and thereafter I never had any qualms of whistling Dixie. In this case, I simply asked the cabbie who picked me up at the airport if he knew where I could get a bottle. Silently he drove up to an old shack, rolled down the window, and asked an ancient black man what he had in stock. "Just Canadian," he replied somewhat apologetically. That was fine with me.

My problem was not willpower in the usual sense. My problem rather was that I used my willpower to prove I was the captain of my own soul and the master of my own fate. Cold sobriety filled me with feelings of inadequacy, insecurity and inferiority. But I felt I was "ten feet tall" after some 80 proof had nursed away the hurt of the sober hour. I was omnipotent. I was as good as the next guy until alcohol let me down with a thud.

This is the real significance of the first step. It forces the alcoholic to abandon all pretense of omnipotence. It says he isn't going anywhere until he "hits bottom." It promises victory through defeat. It assures him that a Power outside himself is ready, willing, and able to help him the minute he is willing to admit that he is powerless to help himself. St. Paul put it like this: "I take pleasure in infirmities . . . for when I am weak, then am I strong" (II Corinthians 12: 10).

Isn't this after all a basic presupposition of Christian theology? We say that a man or woman must surrender all sense of false pride if he or she is to know the reality of Christ. Some psychologists have discovered the wisdom of this Biblical insight when they insist that a person can recover from alcoholism only when he experiences ego reduction at depth. The Church says surrender. Alcoholics Anonymous speaks of hitting bottom. And psychologists talk of the need for the deflation of the ego. But all are basically saying the same thing—an insight which can be incorporated into the life of anyone who is living in organized confusion and quiet desperation.

However, Dr. John E. Keller, chaplain for the Foundation for Human Ecology, Park Ridge, Illinois, and a Lutheran authority on alcohol addiction, has pointed out that the necessary act of surrender is unconscious and cannot be brought about by the will of the patient. He says this psychological phenomenon offers a striking parallel to what the Bible refers to as grace.

Keller's psychotheological insights have been greatly influenced by the work of psychiatrist Harry S. Tiebout, a long-time friend of A.A., who has contributed greatly to our understanding of this complex disease through the publication of such learned tomes as "Surrender Versus Compliance in Therapy," and "The Ego Factors in Surrender in Alcoholism." Basically, Tiebout has discovered that the alcoholic more often than not suffers from what he calls the "King Complex." As the king's will cannot be frustrated, so too the alcoholic defends his hypersensitive ego by flights into grandiosity. But, come to think about it, I know a lot of nonalcoholics who display this same brand of emotional immaturity.

At any rate, Tiebout once wrote an article, "Alcoholics Anonymous—An Experiment of Nature," in which he contrasted the feelings of a woman alcoholic before and after surrender. Her testimony should have obvious parallels for those who have undergone a genuine Christian experience:

Before I felt . . .	After I felt . . .	I have learned the meaning of humility and meditation
unstable	at peace	
tense	safe	
nervous	composed	
afraid	relaxed	
guilty	contented	
ashamed	thankful	
pushed	cleansed	
incapable	sane	
uncertain	receptive	
unworthy	prayerful	
dismayed		

It is at just this point that many evangelicals find it hard to support A.A.'s program for recovery. And the second, third and eleventh steps do nothing to mitigate their fears that A.A. is too inclusivistic and incapable of leading a person to a knowledge of Jesus Christ:

2. Came to believe that a Power greater than ourselves could restore us to sanity.

3. Made a decision to turn our will and our lives over

to the care of God *as we understood Him.*

11. Sought through prayer and meditation to improve our conscious contact with God *as we understood Him,* praying only for knowledge of His will for us and the power to carry that out.

It certainly doesn't help matters for Christians from orthodox traditions to hear rumors that A.A. says it's all right for the recovering alcoholic to make the group—or even a radiator—his Higher Power. I know that I personally had grave doubts about A.A.'s "God-given program" when I contrasted its seemingly all-embracing Higher Power with the fundamentalist deity of my boyhood. Yet the day was to come in my own life when a psychiatrist was to inquire about my concept of God. In my alcoholic fog, I didn't know if he was talking about the so-called Man Upstairs or the man in the moon. Whatever God I once embraced, I thought, had surely let me down. My only god was alcohol.

I was not alone. So many A.A. friends were later to confide in me that they just "couldn't dig the spiritual part of the program." Many from Roman Catholic backgrounds still burned with growing hostility toward the Church of their childhood for implanting within them the concept of a God of wrath. It has always been a source of irony for me to learn that so many scientific studies have shown a direct correlation between alcoholism and a rigid orthodoxy which views alcohol as the forbidden fruit.

This may well explain why so many alcoholics want nothing to do with the Church. I know that I never received a nicer backhanded compliment than the night a pert little Southern belle walked over to me at an A.A. meeting and sweetly drawled: "Ah generally don't like men of the cloth, but ah like you."

Alcoholics Anonymous itself remains aloof from any internecine strife within the field of alcoholism rehabilitation. It "does not wish to engage in any controversy, (and) neither endorses nor opposes any causes." It abides by its own motto: "Live and let live."

Alcoholics Anonymous insists that it is not a religious program. But it does suggest that there are spiritual aspects to recovery. It doesn't promote the pet dogmas of any sect. But it does encourage its members to turn their lives and wills over to the care of a loving God.

But the first task is to get the sick alcoholic sober. A man or woman who has been fleeing from the Hound of Heaven for years isn't about to listen to arguments, based though they may be on the Bible, while his shaking, sweating body is disgorging vomit and his mind calls for another drink. As A.A. says, "First things first."

It has been estimated that as many as fifty percent enter into the A.A. fellowship as atheists or agnostics. Yet almost every member eventually comes to believe in and depend upon the power of a personal God in his life. "In A.A.," its late cofounder Bill W. once wrote, "it has been said that practically no full recovery from alcoholism has been possible without this all-important faith." Moreover, the fact that so many enter the program with little or no faith dispels the notion that A.A. works only for the "religiously susceptible."

John Keller, whose theological orthodoxy is not suspect, has perhaps put A.A.'s spiritual aspect in its proper perspective. He admits that some Christians might be turned off by the "watered down" concept of God within the fellowship. However, he writes:

. . . Actually the more time a person spends with alcoholics and the more time he studies and experiences A.A., the more he is amazed at the content and arrangement of the Twelve Steps together with the careful, excellent choice of key words. They truly bear the "marks of inspiration." Important also is the realization that A.A. is not and does not claim to be a church or a religion. This is not another "way of salvation" that is being offered to people. Their fellowship does not exist to meet this greatest need of man. This need is to be met in the fellowship of the Church, to which God has entrusted the Word and the Sacraments.

I can cite my own experience in support of Dr. Keller's observation. On the one hand, it was A.A. that drove me back to the God of my youth. It made experientially real what I had accepted as theologically correct earlier in my life. On the other hand, I have found as a pastor that A.A. is often used by God as a handmaiden of the Gospel, driving the sick and sorrowing to the Great Physician, Jesus Christ, the author and finisher of our faith. I shall never forget the night I sat in a closed meeting and heard one of our oldtimers casually recite Ephesians 2: 8, 9: "For by grace are ye saved through faith; and that not of yourselves: it is the gift of God: Not of works, lest any man should boast." I had heard those words a thousand times. But that night they burned like live coals in my heart. As one A.A. member so aptly put it, "Alcoholics Anonymous didn't open the gates of Heaven and let me in; but it did open the gates of hell and let me out."

But A.A. didn't only help me to surrender and to place my life and will in the care of Jesus Christ, who, for me, is God, *as I understand Him*. Rather it also gave me a program for daily living. Steps four through ten demanded that I make an initial and continuing "fearless moral inventory" of my life, admitting to God the exact nature of my wrongs, and humbly asking Him to remove my shortcomings and "all these defects of character."

Someone has said that confession is good for the soul. This is particularly true for the alcoholic. Therefore, A.A. asks a new member to get honest. To stop rationalizing excuses for drinking. To stop lying, cheating, stealing, philandering, or doing anything else that inevitably leads to a drink. Members of the fellowship know that a person can never hang on to sobriety, much less find serenity in his new way of life, until he "gets the monkey off the back." Psychology speaks of the need for catharsis. Preachers talk of confession. Alcoholics Anonymous simply suggests that the new member begin to be honest with himself.

However, honesty is not meant to be brutal or self-defeating. Therefore, A.A. counsels the new member not to try to make amends "when to do so would injure . . . others." For example, few wives want to hear the sexual indiscretions of a drunken husband. Nor is it advisable to write a letter to a newly-married former mistress, asking for her understanding and forgiveness.

But you do have to get even these monkeys off your back. Therefore, at the proper time and in the proper place, A.A. suggests that the new member "take the fifth," that is, seek out some close confidant who will listen to his story in a spirit of compassion and confidentiality. That person may be his sponsor or his pastor. But he will be an individual who can withhold judgment and show mercy to a man who bares his soul. While A.A. counsels the new member to exercise discretion in choosing such a confidant, it recognizes that release from this burden can be liberating—and can keep a man from picking up another drink.

One thing A.A. does not do is to tell a person to take someone else's "fearless moral inventory." It doesn't do the alcoholic any good whatever to blame his wife, his boss, or his lot in life for his aberrant drinking. We can't change other people. We can only change ourselves. If we think otherwise, we end up with resentment and self-pity—two of the most destructive emotions which can only lead to another drink.

A corollary to this point: honesty demands that the alcoholic stop finding excuses for his drinking. There may be many excuses, but there are no good reasons.

There is no problem that a drink will not make worse.

This "fearless moral inventory" isn't meant to lead the alcoholic into deeper despair or into a greater loss of self-esteem. He is rather encouraged to make a list of his assets as well as his liabilities. He may be so hung over in guilt, remorse, and fear by the time he comes to A.A. that he is no longer able to see all of the good qualities that were lost in a drunken fog. Every man has many good points on which he can begin to rebuild his shattered life. He should capitalize on them, but no longer to his own self-aggrandizement. Rather in gratitude to God for his newfound sobriety, for gratitude is the key to serenity.

It is on the basis of this "spiritual awakening" that the A.A. member is ultimately led to take the twelfth step by carrying his message of hope to other alcoholics who still suffer. Unfortunately, there are a few within our fellowship that we call "two steppers." They admit they are powerless over alcohol and they are willing to "twelve step" another brother. But they fail to practice all of A.A.'s other principles in all of their affairs. Any newcomer would do well to avoid such people as sponsors. "Stick with the winners," we always say.

John was a winner. He had many years of good sobriety behind him when he made his way into our hearts and home that day so long ago. He not only talked A.A., he lived A.A. He tried to separate cold fact from my alcoholic fancies. He brought me to meeting after meeting. He encouraged Myrt when I had driven her to despair. He picked me up at Newark airport when I had to be poured off the plane. He made out my income tax when I couldn't even look at the forms for fear that I was going to sink deeper into the financial hole. But there was one thing he didn't do: He didn't go out and get drunk simply because his pigeon had let him down. That was *my* problem and it was one he couldn't afford to make his.

What John was came to mean far more to me than

what John actually said. In fact, a lot of what John said was unprintable or came after overexposure beneath the Blarney Stone. But he was a happy and devoted father and husband. He was highly respected in his profession and community. Above all, he stayed sober. But he will probably kill me for saying all these nice things about him.

However, it wasn't until my A.A. anniversary last year that John taught me the most important lesson of all. As my guest speaker, he revealed that something so traumatic occurred in his own life a couple of years ago that he momentarily thought of a drink for a split second. It pointed up the fact that sobriety doesn't mean an end to normal human problems. "I'm still sober only for today," he added. "But I think that I can finally say that I've taken my last drink."

Not only did John's example make an indelible impression on me even in my worst hours; but my introduction to A.A. spoiled my drinking for the sodden years ahead. I now knew what was right. I knew that I could never safely drink again. I knew that alcohol was poison for me. It would lead me to either a mental hospital or an early death. At the very least, it could take away my family, my job, and my self-respect.

One incident occurred after my introduction to A.A. which still amuses me no end. I always hated air travel even though it was an integral part of my life. Consequently, I arrived at the airport early enough to get loaded in one of the airline clubs to which I belonged. I was flying higher than a kite even before I left the ground. Such was the case one day when I left New York for Chicago. However, I became remorseful while in flight and then began to concoct a grandiose scheme of how the airlines could protect us drunks from ourselves.

Accordingly, I made my way with some difficulty to a United reservations counter after landing at Chicago's

O'Hare terminal. "I want to speak to the manager," I announced with a distinct slur.

"Can I help you, sir?" the clerk inquired.

"No," said I. "I'm an alcoholic and I want to see the manager."

Now there's an introduction that will get quick action. The United reservations supervisor immediately appeared on the scene and led me to a soft chair in his office. "What can I do for you?" he asked.

I allowed that there were probably hundreds like me who get bombed before sailing into the wild, blue yonder; and I suggested that the airlines ought to get together and provide coffee, etc. for poor souls like me. The man listened to my tale of woe with great compassion, explaining the difficulties the airlines would face if they set up a special program for alcoholics. He was a really nice guy, and I felt much better as I left his office to quench a thirst that was fast becoming unbearable.

But there's a postscript to this story. Any alcoholic looking for friends can now attend an A.A. meeting any time he happens to fly into John F. Kennedy airport in New York on Monday, Wednesday or Friday. The group meets at noon in the beautiful Protestant chapel.

Most of my drunk-a-logue was anything but funny. There were the gigantic telephone bills that I ran up when I suddenly decided to call my wife in some far-off port at three o'clock in the morning. There were those times when I was forced to knock out a news story with fingers that were all thumbs. There were also occasions when I wallowed in fear for missing an assignment altogether.

So bad was my condition becoming that I had to use every ounce of that misplaced willpower to achieve even the slightest goal. I remember one day in Dixie when I somehow managed to research a magazine piece that was supposed to be phoned in to my editor in Philadelphia at nine o'clock the next morning. However, I left my news sources to get a much-needed bracer. Of course, it didn't stop there, and I knew I was in no condition to try to write that evening. Instead, I sacked in at my hotel, having the good sense to have the clerk awaken me at five the next morning. I got up with the appointed ring, poured a water tumbler of whiskey, and then tried my best to hammer out a lead. It took another tumbler of whiskey, but I did phone in that story precisely on the dot of nine. What I didn't know was that my editor was listening to the transcription of my masterpiece—"Shhh as in Shhamuel . . ." "You're not feeling too good," he remarked, as I signed off with a 30 and good-bye. I wasn't. I needed another drink.

Where did I go wrong?

A lot of my trouble after my introduction to A.A. involved the fact that I thought I was *too young* to be an alcoholic. It is true that men and women older than myself formed a majority in the fellowship when I first became a member. But now, as the disease concept of alcoholism becomes better known, we even find teenagers turning up at the door of A.A. worried about a drinking problem.

Coupled with the argument of youth was my iron determination to *analyze* rather than *utilize*. Some professionals have a harder time adapting to the A.A. way of life because their training always led them back to the matter of causality. I wanted to know what made me an alcoholic—if I really suffered from an incurable disease. It took a long time for me to get it through my thick skull that I could never return to so-called normal social drinking. Anyone who must *prove* to his own satisfaction whether he has crossed that invisible line might try this experiment: Take any number of drinks—say, three or four—and make that your daily limit for a given period. If you go beyond that number *for any reason,* you have flunked the most important test of your life!

Still another problem involved my tendency to *compare* rather than to *identify* with A.A. friends. I knew I wasn't like the big construction worker who drank himself into oblivion on Aqua Velva. I had ended up in only one hospital; but I had never been arrested or committed to a mental institution. I still hung on to my family and job by the skin of my teeth. I hadn't lost my health or my entire reputation. "So none of these things ever happened to you," A.A. friends remarked. "Well, keep on drinking and they will." I kept on drinking, and some of them did.

What probably hurt me the most was my king-sized ego. Those "abominable" A.A. cliches were an insult to my intelligence: *Live and Let Live . . . First Things First . . . Think.* And that sign, *But for the Grace of God.* Who were these drunks to tell me, a budding Tillich or Barth, about *sola gratia* or *sola fide?* And so I continued to demonstrate my genius by getting drunk.

I was something like a pigeon of my own that I was later to take to Mount Carmel. He was quite proper and well-to-do, and he insisted upon dressing up in a new suit, shirt, tie, and hat for his ride to the hospital. But the only way I could get him there was to let him continue drinking during the long trip. When we finally arrived, I asked a couple of guys to help me get him into the place since he was quite incapable of getting there under his own steam. My once-dignified pigeon slowly moved his bulky frame out of the door. And new suit or not, his pants promptly fell to the ground!

I saw myself in him that day, beating my head against a wall for years, until I at last came crashing to the ground with a thud.

3

The God of the Preachers

*"Jesus (said), Verily, verily, I say unto thee,
Except a man be born of water and of the
Spirit, he cannot enter into the kingdom of
God. That which is born of the flesh is flesh;
and that which is born of the Spirit is spirit.
Marvel not that I said unto thee, Ye must be
born again"* (John 3: 5-7).

FOUR BIG, FRIENDLY ARMS reached out as my liquor-lean
body crumpled to the sidewalk in midtown Manhattan
during the height of the lunch hour. Two burly men,
whose compassion may well have been born out of a similar experience, joked about my sodden condition so early
in the day. Then they carried me into a nearby bar to
sober up.

The bartender didn't like the idea one bit. But he
let me sit there in an alcoholic fog after my unknown
benefactors snapped back at him, "Tough! He probably
got his load in here."

That really was not the case. I had been on a one-
night drinking spree, following what turned out to be a
minor frustration in life. I drank far into the night and
then waited for the liquor store to open the next morning
so that I could buy a half pint of gin to finish off the

job. I drank it down straight. And that was the last thing I remembered until I found myself as the unwelcome guest in a gin mill.

As the fog began to clear, I felt a fresh flush of guilt and remorse for letting my family down once more. I knew the danger from past experience of attempting to get home in my condition. There had been times when I was roused into consciousness by a bus driver at the last stop in the dead of night. But this time there was an angel at my shoulder, and somehow I made it all the way home.

Myrt said nothing when she arrived home that evening to find me in a restless sleep. She had been through it all so many times before. So she simply went about making supper for herself and the boys. And for me.

That supper, though no one knew it then, was to figure prominently in my recovery. It consisted of meatloaf, tomatoes poured over mashed potatoes, and chopped fresh spinach. It was my idea of a gourmet's delight. It was my favorite meal.

I made a feeble but genuine effort to get a few bites of solid food into my shrunken stomach. Then I went downstairs to face my wife and children, moving at the same time toward the refrigerator to pull out a half-gallon jug of wine. "Oh, no!" cried Myrt in desperation.

"Honey," I pleaded sheepishly. "I just need this one drink to see me through the night."

Myrt was unimpressed. But the next morning I poured the remainder of that wine down the kitchen sink. I had taken my last drink.

There were no flashes in the sky. But somehow I knew that something radical had occurred within me. I had thrown in the sponge. I was tired, so very tired, of fighting John Barleycorn. The things I had learned from John and at Mount Carmel began to make sense. The old Paul, with all of his pretensions of omnipotence, had died. And the reality of my rebirth assumed an almost sacramental nature as the old suit, ripped in the fall of the day before, was unceremoniously thrown into the garbage can.

I still am—and always will be—one drink away from a drunk. In order to retain my prized sobriety, I must work the A.A. program one day at a time. I must "keep my memory green" through active participation in my A.A. group. That means identification with other A.A. members and the willingness to share my experience, strength and hope with the alcoholic who still suffers. For the price of liberty is eternal vigilance.

Many nonalcoholics find such a perspective for daily living either stifling or debilitating. They suggest that the A.A. member and his family sit on a powder keg that threatens to blow up at any minute. But are we any different from the person with diabetes? We, like them, suffer from a progressive disease which cannot be cured —but can be controlled. It might be stifling and debilitating for the diabetic to live under the strict regimen of diet and insulin. But would anyone suggest that the diabetic abandon this regimen, knowing that his life depends upon it? Similarly, A.A. is the alcoholic's medicine. To neglect to take it in massive doses can mean insanity or death. "Wherefore let him that thinketh he standeth take heed lest he fall" (I Corinthians 10: 12).

An alcoholic might be able to remain dry outside A.A. for long periods of time. But it is extremely doubtful that he will ever find serenity in sobriety outside the A.A. fellowship. Some alcoholics only manage to "stay on the wagon" by the skin of their teeth. They are on continual "dry drunks," making life miserable for themselves and their families as they continue to wrestle with that psychological craving for that illusive "safe" drink. Alcoholics Anonymous simply helps us to deal realistically with such fantasies, and, at the same time, enjoy ourselves while doing so; A.A. makes the going great!

This does not mean that the normal emotional problems of living suddenly disappear the minute the alcoholic crosses the threshold of A.A. There are constitutional and psychological factors which we carry into sobriety, as well as infantile religious hangups which impede our spiritual and emotional growth. But A.A. gives us the tools with which to work on these "defects of character" and encourages us to stop thinking that we are wise enough or strong enough to solve all of our problems in solitary misery. We are taught, rather, to lean on the group for strength and to "let go and let God."

Alcoholics Anonymous works for those who want it to work. But experience has shown that half measures avail nothing. It is one thing to be *around* A.A. It is another thing entirely to be *in* A.A. Therefore, we are not merely told to "put the cork in the bottle"—but to be honest with ourselves. If a man wants to drink, A.A. will not try to stop him. But if he has "hit bottom," A.A. will show him the path to recovery.

Our fellowship promises nothing but sobriety. We don't pass out dollars for indigent drunks. Nor do we run an employment agency or a marriage counseling service. We don't try to change anyone but ourselves. "Our primary purpose is to stay sober and to help other alcoholics achieve sobriety." A better job or a better marriage is simply the frosting on the cake—the fringe benefits of remaining faithful to our one primary goal.

Alcoholics Anonymous demands "costly discipleship." Our very willingness to "twelve step" another drunk whom the world has forgotten attests to our utter belief in the Master's words: "He that findeth his life shall lose it: and he that loseth his life for my sake shall find it. He that receiveth you receiveth me, and he that receiveth me receiveth him that sent me" (Matthew 10: 39, 40).

It is precisely at this point that many Christians find

it difficult to square their own religious convictions with those of A.A. They believe that the alcoholic should be led to a definite commitment for Christ. The psychiatrist takes a similar tack by insisting that something be done about the alcoholic's underlying personality disorder.

Such rigidity of outlook recalls the story of the child psychiatrist who captivated audiences by recommending that children be allowed to develop in a largely permissive atmosphere. No threats. No paddling. No punishment of any kind. Accordingly, one couple was so impressed that they brought their unmanageable youngster in to see this highly touted miracle work. Whereupon the psychiatrist gave the boy a hard slap across his face. In shocked disbelief, the father asked: "Is that what you mean by therapeutic?" "No," replied the doctor. "But I have to get his attention before I can do anything with him."

That's the way it generally is with the alcoholic. He has conned both preachers and psychiatrists. So A.A. strives to get him sober before it tries to reason with him in increasing doses. And, while A.A. has no argument with either religion or psychiatry, the statistics show that it has helped more drunks recover from alcoholism than any other type of therapy.

It worked in my case when all other avenues of hope eventually came to a dead end. Neither a warmly evangelical upbringing nor a Christian college and seminary were able to keep me from the ravages of alcoholism. In fact, I was thoroughly demoralized and in abject despair when I returned to the Christ of my youth through the A.A. fellowship.

My theological roots lie buried deep within the Calvinist tradition. But I no longer theorize about such doctrines as unconditional election, irresistible grace or the eternal security of the believer. For theory has now been validated by reality. And I claim John Newton's thrilling testimony as my own:

> Through many dangers, toils and snares,
>   I have already come;
> 'Tis grace hath brought me safe thus far,
>   And grace will lead me home.

There is not the slightest doubt in my mind today that my conversion experience was real that night many years ago when, as a teenager, I walked to the front of the auditorium of Town Hall in New York City to receive Jesus Christ as Savior, if not as Lord. Indeed, I am now convinced that my divine Elder Brother left the Father's House to pursue me into the far country, there to lead me home when I finally came to my senses (Luke 15: 11-32).

Other Christians may find it difficult—if not impossible—to reconcile the use of spirits with the Spirit-changed life. For St. Paul declared: "If any man be in Christ, he is a new creature: old things are passed away; behold, all things are become new" (II Corinthians 5: 17). All I can say in light of this blessed truth is that the blood was *applied* that night in Town Hall, but it was not fully *appropriated* until many years later.

This fact was driven home to me recently as I counseled a young woman on the verge of taking her life. She had accepted Christ after numerous experiments with LSD and other mind-altering drugs. She simply did not *feel* saved. It was only after God Himself challenged her to forget her *feelings* and simply accept the *fact* of salvation that her outlook on life began to brighten a bit.

Yet I and a lot of other Christians have been just like this young woman. We confuse outward circumstance with an inward spiritual reality. We allow an environment made hostile by family or friends to serve as a barometer of our standing in Christ. For we have not yet learned to appropriate the words of the hymnwriter into our own hearts:

Though the angry surges roll
On my tempest-driven soul,
I am peaceful, for I know,
Wildly though the winds may blow,
I've an anchor safe and sure,
That can evermore endure.
And it holds . . .
My anchor holds!

William James, the great experimental psychologist, reflected my own spiritual immaturity when he wrote of why men turn to alcohol. "The sway of alcohol over mankind," he said, "is unquestionably due to its power to stimulate the mystical faculties of human nature, usually crushed to earth by the cold facts and dry criticisms of the sober hour."

I know of only one "social drink" in my life. I took it at five years of age when a somewhat *bon vivant* uncle took me into a men's bar for lunch while my mother and his wife went shopping at Gimbels. He ordered a ham on rye and a beer. I ordered the same.

That was my one and only "social drink." From then on, I drank only for the effect. I wanted to blot out "the cold facts and dry criticisms of the sober hour." For I grew into a very insecure adolescent, ashamed of my weak frame and unable to cope with peer pressures. It always seemed as though I was the odd man out. Or the man who wasn't there at all.

Yet I had tremendous drive and an insatiable curiosity. The latter quality proved to be both an asset and a liability in my emotional development. My curiosity heightened my feelings of rejection in the strict fundamentalist circles of my youth. For doctrines, no matter how poorly stated, were to be believed rather than questioned. Consequently, my drive for a reasonable faith earned me only the reputation of being somewhat akin to a Marxist revisionist. I had become a theological pariah as a teenager—a time in my life when inwardly I cried for the fellowship of the Church.

But my drive and my curiosity also proved to be an asset. For without them I never would have landed my first newspaper job. My old city editor later informed me that the only reason he hired me was to get rid of me. I pounded on his door regularly until he agreed to hire me as a cub reporter out in the boondocks. Six weeks later, I covered my first murder and was moved to the city staff. I held the top reportorial slot, the City Hall beat, when I was 19 years old.

The Fourth Estate bandaged a bruised ego with my first tastes of glory. I had not been able to compete with other kids on the football field or on the Sing-spiration circuit. But I had achieved a temporary sense of self-esteem that no one else could claim. For who among my peers had ever felt the joy I experienced that night when I got a call on city desk. It was the district attorney. He had called to let me know that his men had just arrested the chief of police and the head of the vice squad. Silently my city editor got up and moved quickly to that button on the wall. He stopped the presses so that we could replate page one for the next edition. I wrote my story, then headed downstairs to the mail room to await the sight of my byline in 10 point bold caps on the lead story on page one.

Yet my love for the Fourth Estate was tempered by a desire to go to college and begin preparation for the Gospel ministry. We took that plunge on faith—a month after Myrt and I were married in 1950. We had $600 between us and a warning from fellow Christians that there were rumors that our college was "going liberal." All I know is that the tears rolled down my face daily as Terrelle B. Crum, God bless him, answered those questions which previously had been taken as a sign of blatant unbelief.

At the same time, my college years were hard years. Money was so tight that we often debated whether a hamburger would wreck our weekly budget. Myrt had to work even after the birth of our first child, while I managed to scrape up a few dollars as a "stringer" for a national wire service. When that job petered out, I went successively from a janitor in an Episcopal boys school, to a drill press operator in a factory, to a magazine salesman. And all the while I was building up a healthy case of self-pity and resentment, bolstered by some incidents even now too painful to mention.

The final blow came when we lost our babysitter as I was about to enter my final semester. I was an honor student, and Dean Crum, gracious and understanding as always, saw to it that I could complete my last six credits on a seminar basis while I went out job hunting. I quickly found one on a New England radio station, where I manned the swing shift as a reporter-newscaster for the next two years.

My father's death brought me to a newspaper close to home. I loved that saintly man, even though the harsh economic facts of life forced him to be away from the family during those years I needed him most. But whatever pain I felt inside soon washed away in an alcoholic glow. Sober I may have been nothing; but with a few drinks I felt ten feet tall.

I had taken an occasional drink during my precollege newspapering days. In fact, I recall waking up one Sunday morning fully clothed, wondering how I got to my room the night before. I remember being overwhelmed by guilt and remorse. So I headed for church, promising myself that this would never happen again. How wrong I was!

Something was radically different about my entire attitude when I picked up that first drink four days after beginning my stint on that Pennsylvania newspaper. I was thoroughly exhausted—physically weakened and emotionally drained—from a lack of sleep and from covering a flood that raged through the Pocono Mountains, taking the lives of more than seventy people, many of them children.

We had just put the paper to bed after publishing our first postflood editions when I walked into Bill Quick's Bar. Being a novice at this sort of thing, I ordered a beer as I heard a voice shout to the bartender: "Give the skinny one a drink." Through the dim light of the kerosene lamps, I could see the shadowed figure of my managing editor. I was grateful when he invited me to join him at his table. But little did I know then that he would die the tragic death of an alcoholic.

As for me, that drink was my Salk vaccine, my vitamin shot, and my nerve medicine all poured into one elixir of the gods. I vowed then that I would never be without it again. It was to be my daily companion for years to come, at times the source of chemical comfort, but ultimately the forbidden fruit of a man-made hell. At the outset, I lived to drink; but the day came when I drank to live.

I can now look back to see that I was light-years away from what Erik Erikson calls the crisis of adolescence. To my own way of thinking, I may have been an intellectual giant; but, in reality, I was a spiritual and emotional pygmy. I could not accept myself, and consequently I could not accept other people. I had a loving and faithful wife, yet I sought the companionship of people who did not share her concern about my aberrant drinking habits. I may not have caused her any physical pain; but I made up for it in spiritual and emotional abuse beyond measure. For alcoholism is the family disease. It ravages the lives of those nearest and dearest to the alcoholic.

My wife detested the personality change she saw wrought in the man she married. Sober I was quiet, reasonably thoughtful, and deeply in love with my family. But I was arrogant and grandiose—or maudlin and morose—the minute I had downed a few drinks.

Apart from my insecurity, I felt terribly rebellious against the Church and the god who let me down. A fire raged within over the real or imagined abuses I had suffered at the hands of fellow Christians. My deepest needs had not been met within the fellowship of the Church. But, so what, I thought, as the pain was drowned by another drink.

Somewhere along the way there had also been a gradual shift in my sense of values. I remember how guilty I sometimes felt in college when our own economic needs forced me to sell magazines to families that could have better used the money for food and clothing. Lying, cheating, and stealing became a way of life. I came to see that I was a phony and that any pretensions of a spiritual life were now hypocritical and counterfeit.

Yet there was that deep conviction that seminary would alter my incredible capacity for alcohol. I quite literally began my preparation for the ministry as a means of finding victory over Demon Rum.

But I was like so many other alcoholics whom I have since come to meet. I prayed earnestly to God for deliverance even while I was picking up the next drink. What I really wanted was a safe drinking formula, not total freedom from alcohol. I had not yet learned that I had crossed that invisible line between social and compulsive drinking, that half measures would avail me nothing. I was hooked, the victim of a physical allergy coupled with a mental obsession.

It was only after I fell on my face in midtown Manhattan that I threw in the sponge. I had no other choice but to let go and let God. I was a beaten man. And there were times in the days and months which followed that I could barely put one foot in front of the other. But A.A. friends promised me that "this too shall pass." They were right, and finally the day came when the joy of Charles Wesley's words burst alive within me:

My chains fell off,
  My heart was free;
I rose, went forth,
  And followed Thee.

So often now I am led to close my talk before A.A. groups with the ringing testimony of Martin Luther King, Jr., "Free at last, free at last. Thank God Almighty, I'm free at last!" And yet the knowledge that I will always be just one drink from a drunk demands that I temper that testimony by paraphrasing the words of the great hymn of the civil rights movement:

I can overcome,
  I can overcome *today;*
Deep in my heart,
  I do believe,
I can overcome *today!*

That is my story. Each A.A. member has his own to tell. We come from different walks in life. We all have had different life experiences and varied drinking patterns. But we are united in a fellowship of love and mutual concern in which we seek not to compare but to identify with one another.

Yet the miracle of a spiritual rebirth has figured prominently in so many A.A. success stories. Bill W., our beloved cofounder, emphasized this fact when he testified before a Senate subcommittee on alcoholism and narcotics shortly before his death in 1970.

Bill told that subcommittee, headed by a senator who is himself a recovered alcoholic, that later reflection showed that A.A. was actually born in the Zurich office of

Carl Gustav Jung, one of the great pioneers in modern psychiatry.

Dr. Jung had been treating a patient known in A.A. history as Roland H. He was a prominent American businessman who had turned to the celebrated Swiss psychiatrist as a court of last resort in his battle with the bottle. In the year that he spent in Zurich, he came to love Dr. Jung, and, at the same time, learn much about those personality traits which had in the past triggered so many drunks.

It was in the early 1930s that Roland left Zurich with the profound hope that he had mastered his problem. But he returned to Dr. Jung within a month, following another disastrous episode with alcohol. "Karl," he asked, "what does this all mean?"

Bill told the senators that it was his own personal conviction that Dr. Jung's answer to that agonizing question led to the eventual establishment of Alcoholics Anonymous. "Roland," said Jung, "up until recently I thought you might be one of those rare cases who could be aided and made to recover by the practice of my art. But like most who will pass through here, I must confess that my art can do nothing for you."

"What?" said the patient. "Doctor, you are my court of last resort. Where shall I turn now? Is there no other recourse?"

Jung thought silently for a moment. "Yes," he said finally, "there may be. There is the off chance. I am speaking to you of the possibility of a spiritual awakening —a conversion, if you like."

"Oh," replied Roland somewhat skeptically. "But I am a religious man. I used to be a vestryman in the Episcopal Church. I still have faith in God. But I think He has little faith in me."

Jung shook his head. "Roland," he said, "I mean something that goes deeper than that—not just a question of faith. I am talking about a transforming of spirit that can remotivate you and set you free . . .

"Time after time alcoholics have recovered by these means," he continued. "The lightning strikes here and there, and no one can say why or how. All I can suggest is that you expose yourself to some religious environment of your own choice."

A close personal friend, a student of Jung and himself a psychiatrist in Zurich, has told me that his distinguished mentor was not personally a religious man, although he recognized its healing effect for many patients. Whatever the case, Jung's advice to Roland represents a modern-day replication of that confrontation long ago when the Great Physician informed another man who was spiritually sick: "You must be born again."

Roland took his doctor's advice. He went to England where he became interested in the Oxford Group Movement, then at the height of its popularity in Europe. It had won hundreds with its tenets of absolute purity, absolute honesty, absolute unselfishness, and absolute love, as well as by its stress on self-survey, confession, restitution and prayer. While the movement lost the support of many evangelicals, it was within its fellowship that Roland found release and returned to America a free man.

While regaining his strength at home in Vermont, Roland ran into a friend of Bill W. His name was Edwin T. (Ebby of A.A. fame), who was about to be committed to a mental institution because of his drinking.

Bill was unable to hide a slight smile as he told the senators of the time Ebby had driven his car through the kitchen wall of an old New England farmhouse. "When he stopped," Bill recalled, "out stepped a horrified lady, who asked, 'How about a cup of coffee?' "

It wasn't long after this incident that Roland witnessed to Ebby about his own spiritual rebirth. He told of his own failures as long as he sought deliverance by his own unaided human resources. He encouraged him to turn over his life and will to the care of a loving God. Ebby did. And promptly he sobered up.

Then Ebby learned that Bill, an old school chum turned stockbroker, had been given up by his physician as a hopeless alcoholic. In fact, Dr. William D. Silkworth had sadly informed Bill's wife: "Lois, I am afraid, my dear, that I can do nothing. I thought that he might be one of those rare instances in which I could help him stay sober. But I am afraid not. He is the victim of a compulsion to drink against his will. And, as much as he desires it, I don't think that compulsion can be broken."

"Silky," as he was to become known to hundreds of AA's, then dropped his medical bombshell. "Lois," he said, "I think you will have to lock him up."

However, that now white-haired darling took her tragically-ill husband home once more. Bill was sitting at the kitchen table with a big pitcher of gin and pineapple juice when Ebby suddenly knocked at the door.

By this time, Bill was a solitary drinker, consuming two or three bottles of bathtub gin a day. He had become a loner, and, except for Lois, his only friend was booze. But he was glad to see Ebby, whom, he informed the senators, "I had known to be a very hopeless case."

Ebby told Bill of his own spiritual awakening. In essence, he informed his friend that (1) he admitted that he was powerless to help himself, (2) that he had honestly examined his conscience, (3) that he had made a rigorous confession of his personal defects of character, (4) that he had sought to make amends to those he had hurt, (5) that he resolved to serve others without thought of personal prestige or material gain, and (6) that he was now seeking God's will for his life.

To Bill, this formula sounded markedly naive. But

years later, in writing to Dr. Jung about this encounter, he recalled:

> I had long marked my friend Edwin for a hopeless case. Yet here he was in a very evident state of "release" which could by no means be accounted for by his mere association for a very short time with the Oxford groups. Yet this obvious state of release, as distinguished from the usual depression, was tremendously convincing. Because he was a kindred sufferer, he could unquestionably communicate with me at great depth. I knew at once I must find an experience like his—or die.

Bill could not forget that face across the kitchen table. "Yet I gagged on this concept of a Higher Power," he said, "even in its lowest denominator." He completely rejected any notion of what he termed an "emotional conversion."

But something *was* happening inside Bill. He told Dr. Silkworth as much when he again entered Towns Hospital in New York City a month after Ebby's initial visit. He had been in detoxification for about three days when suddenly he was gripped in a depression, unlike anything he had ever experienced before. He felt trapped. Tears rolled down his bloated cheeks as he cried out: "If there is a God, let Him show Himself! I am ready to do anything! Anything!"

That cry of surrender was to be my own years later. But let Bill tell in his own words what happened next:

> "Suddenly the room lit up with a great white light. I was caught up into an ecstasy which there are no words to describe. It seemed to me, in the mind's eye, that I was on a mountain and that a wind not of air but of spirit was blowing. And then it burst upon me that I was a free man. Slowly the ecstasy subsided. I lay on the bed, but now for a time I was in another world, a new world of consciousness. All about me and through me there was a wonderful feeling of Presence, and I thought to myself, 'So this is

the God of the preachers.' A great peace stole over me and I thought, 'No matter how wrong things seem to be, they are still all right. Things are all right with God and His world.' "[1]

In time, Bill came to realize that not all alcoholics would share so dramatic a spiritual transformation. However, this discovery did not come until after he failed miserably in his efforts to effect a wholesale cure of fellow drunks by playing the role of an evangelist. It was then that Dr. Silkworth offered his advice: "Give them the medical business, and give it to them hard," he said. "Skip that account of your hot flash." So Bill shifted his emphasis from sin to sickness. And things began to look up.

The turning point in his "divine appointment" came about six months after his miraculous confrontation with "the God of the preachers." He had gone to Akron, Ohio, to attempt to rebuild his financial fences. But he lost a proxy fight and ended up with hardly more than carfare home. "All of a sudden the old desire to drink started to come back," he recalled. "I was frightened."

However, his eye caught sight of a church directory hanging in the lobby across from the hotel bar. Suddenly, he felt the urge to call an Episcopal clergyman to see if he could put him in contact with another alcoholic. That was the only way he knew to stay sober.

The result was that Bill met Dr. Bob, who had virtually lost his medical practice because of this disease without a cure. The date was Mother's Day, 1935, and Dr. Bob had returned home earlier that day lugging an expensive potted plant, which he placed on the kitchen table. He then passed out.

This time Bill did not preach. "I just talked away about my own case," he recalled, "until (Dr. Bob) got a good identification with me, until he began to say, 'Yes, that's me. I'm like that.' " The outcome was that A.A.'s second cofounder stopped drinking almost immediately and remained sober until his death in 1950.

Both men immediately began working with other alcoholics at Akron's City Hospital, where one patient quickly achieved complete sobriety. It was this trio which formed the nucleus of the first A.A. group, although the name of the fellowship had not yet been coined. However, Bill said later, this "idea of mutual need added the final ingredient to the synthesis of medicine, religion, and the alcoholic's experience, which is now Alcoholics Anonymous."

In the Fall of 1935, a second group of alcoholics slowly took shape in New York City. A third appeared in Cleveland in 1939. It had taken more than four years to produce one hundred sober alcoholics in the three founding groups.

Those early years were filled with monumental frustration and suffering for the men and women who had just escaped from the inner precincts of hell. One has only to read Bill's account of those pioneering days in *Alcoholics Anonymous Comes of Age* to realize that only a miracle-working God can explain the gradual—then explosive—growth of this unlikely kinship of suffering.

There were the ego trips, the petty squabbles that led some back to the bottle. There were also those intermittent temptations to appeal to the wealthy so that A.A. could go professional. But it was out of these frustrations that the infant fellowship hammered out some of its time-honored traditions: Self-support through the contributions of its own members, nonalliance with any outside causes, personal anonymity at the level of press, radio and films, a public relations policy based upon attraction rather than promotion, and the commitment to principles rather than personalities.

Alcoholics Anonymous found it necessary early in its history to break completely from the Oxford Group

Movement. It did so because many alcoholics rebelled against the organization's aggressive evangelism, the principle of "team guidance," and the concept of absolutes. They just wanted to gain sobriety and were not interested in getting "too good too soon." But Bill pointed to yet another difficulty:

> "Because of the stigma then attached to the condition, most alcoholics wanted to be anonymous. We were afraid also of developing erratic public characters who, through broken anonymity, might get drunk in public and so destroy confidence in us. The Oxford Groups, on the contrary, depended very much upon the use of prominent names—something that was doubtless all right for them but mighty hazardous for us."

Some might seriously question my own motives for remaining as the anonymous author of this book. They might well conclude that I am ashamed of being both an alcoholic and a minister of the Gospel. But quite the contrary is true. I am a proud and grateful alcoholic.

In fact, I am often reminded of the story of a Scottish evangelist by the name of Brownlow North, who had sown his wild oats in his younger days. One Sunday he was handed a letter just as he was about to preach in a church in Aberdeen. The writer revealed that he knew all about Brownlow North's past indiscretions and warned that he would expose him if he dared to preach that day. But that did not deter the evangelist. He took the letter into the pulpit, read its contents to the congregation, and readily admitted that every word was true. However, he added that he had become a new creation in Jesus Christ. And, he asked, if Christ could change him, could He not also change any man or woman burdened by sin, guilt and remorse?

I feel exactly like Brownlow North. I am not proud in the least of my past. But I am deeply proud to be a member of Alcoholics Anonymous and a blood-bought child of God in Christ. Therefore, when I mount my pulpit each Lord's Day morning, not knowing the specific needs of my people, I am at least aware that, if Christ could change me, He can change any man, woman or young person in my congregation. I stand in my pulpit as Exhibit A to prove that human nature can indeed be redeemed!

My anonymity as an alcoholic is restricted only at the level of press, radio and film. My own people are well aware that their pastor was rescued from the far country by a loving God. But if I were to break my anonymity in a book or on a television show, there would always be that possibility that personality would be elevated above principle, that people would see the ex-drunk instead of the God I seek to know, love and serve.

Anonymity at this level assures the alcoholic who still suffers that his own desire for confidentiality will always be respected. It also testifies to the growth of the recovering alcoholic himself. For anonymity crucifies the old "I" which, in the past, led to our downfall. Therefore, we AA's say that anonymity is one of the spiritual bedrocks upon which our fellowship is founded. It means self-effacement rather than self, sacrifice rather than sacrilegious pride.

Little did our pioneers know that a full century before A.A. an organization with similar goals was established in Baltimore, Maryland. It was known as The Washington Temperance Society, and, like A.A., it stressed (1) mutual help among alcoholics, (2) weekly meetings, (3) shared experience, (4) reliance upon a loving God for help, and (5) total abstinence from alcohol. All went along fine for these Washingtonians until they became embroiled in the social and political polemics of their day. When that happened, they faded into oblivion. But they left behind concrete evidence as to the wisdom of

A.A. hewing to that one primary purpose of carrying its message to the alcoholic who still suffers.

This firm resolve may not endear the fellowship to those Christians who believe the cardinal doctrines of the Church should be written into the A.A. program for recovery. Some of the early pioneers tried to do just this very thing. However, Bill and Dr. Bob, both ardent Christians until their deaths, realized that such a course would be self-defeating. While the liberals insisted there could be no agreement in theology, the atheists and agnostics contended that many drunks would be scared away by anything that smacked of religion. "This was the great contribution of our atheists and agnostics," said Bill. "They had widened our gateway so that all who suffer might pass through, regardless of their belief or lack of belief."

Moreover, when you're working with a bunch of drunks, you *suggest* rather than *command*. For alcoholics, long the brunt of threats from a boss or spouse, generally react to orders by going out for another drink. Consequently, there are no Ten Commandments in A.A.—just twelve *suggested* steps for recovery. "We are not bound by theological doctrine," Dr. Bob once remarked. "None of us may be excommunicated and cast into outer darkness. For we are many minds in our organization, and an A.A. decalogue in the language of 'Thou shalt not' would gall us indeed."

This singular emphasis on grace and freedom has always attracted many distinguished evangelical leaders to the A.A. way of life. They have recognized that, while individual members may witness to their Christian faith, the primary responsibility for evangelism belongs to the Church—not Alcoholics Anonymous or any other organization. At the same time, they have seen too many lives changed and brought to God within the A.A. fellowship to be anything but staunch supporters of its miracle-working program. Said one noted clergyman, "I have listened to many learned arguments about God, but for honest-to-goodness experiential evidence of God, His power personally appropriated and His reality indubitably assured, give me a good meeting of A.A.!"

The late Rev. Dr. Samuel Shoemaker, onetime rector of Calvary Episcopal Church, Pittsburgh, went a step further. He once preached a sermon entitled, "What the Church Can Learn From Alcoholics Anonymous." Of course, both Bill W. and Dr. Bob always credited Sam with being "one of the prime sources of influence that have gathered themselves together into what is now A.A."

So great was Dr. Sam's love for A.A.—and A.A.'s love for Dr. Sam—that he counted it a high honor to be mistaken for a member of the fellowship. On one occasion, an A.A. gal asked him if he was an alcoholic. Sam had to admit that he wasn't. "Well," said the girl, "you talk like one!"

We AA's claim that it takes an alcoholic to talk to an alcoholic. So that young woman paid Sam Shoemaker the highest compliment. For unlike so many other Christians, he had sat where we sat.

4

The Thirteenth American

> *"Then these righteous ones will reply, 'Sir,*
> *when did we ever see you hungry and feed*
> *you? Or thirsty and give you anything to*
> *drink? Or a stranger, and help you? Or*
> *naked, and clothe you? When did we ever*
> *see you sick or in prison, and visit you?'*
> *And I, the King, will tell them, 'When you*
> *did it to these my brothers you were doing*
> *it to me!' "* (Matthew 25: 37-40 LB).

THE REV. DR. HERMAN J. KREGEL is a somewhat crusty
retired Army chaplain who likes figures—provided they
show balanced budgets and a reduction in human misery.

But there are some figures that make the director of
the Berkeley Center for Alcoholic Studies boiling mad.
And he'll rip them off at the drop of a hat:

... About half of the nation's annual highway death
toll—involving some 28,000 Americans—are directly related to the use and abuse of beverage alcohol. In some
areas the percentage of alcohol-related fatalities runs as
high as 80 percent of all highway deaths.

... Some 800,000 drinking driver accidents occurred
in 1969 alone, maiming or impairing two million people,
and costing about $6 billion in insurance claims, which
the companies passed on to policy holders in the form of

higher premiums.

. . . Alcohol abuse kills more people, ruins more homes and careers, and causes more losses to our economy than all other drugs combined.

. . . The life expectancy of the problem drinker is 12 years less than that of the general population. Almost half of them die before their fifty-first birthday.

. . . The suicide rate of alcoholics is reported to be fifty times higher than the overall national average.

. . . Drinking has been established as a major cause of the nation's spiraling divorce rate. In 1965, for example, there were 481,000 marriage break-ups—of which 325,000 were attributed to alcohol abuse.

. . . The F.B.I. has estimated that as many as fifty percent of all reported arrests in the United States—exclusive of minor traffic violations—are for alcohol-related offenses.

. . . Private industry loses an estimated $7 billion annually because of alcoholism or alcohol dependence, while the Federal General Accounting Office concluded that the government could save as much as $280 million a year by establishing alcoholism programs for its employees.

If Dr. Kregel's statistics sound sensational, think again.

Religious News Service reported that 43,000 Americans lost their life in a little more than nine years of fighting in Vietnam. In that same period, however, 240,000 persons were killed by drunken drivers.

An official of the U.S. Department of Transportation further dramatized the entire sordid matter by pointing out that there would be an immediate public outcry if the airlines lost a jumbo jet filled with passengers every week. Yet very little is said about the fact that as many people as can be carried on the largest jet die weekly because of alcohol-related slaughter on the highways.

Alcohol addiction appears to be a mounting problem

in many parts of the world. Officials in the Soviet Union were moved to take harsh measures against problem drinkers when it became apparent they were jeopardizing their nation's five-year plan. The Spanish government, remaining somewhat ambivalent because of the country's reputation for wine, is nevertheless deeply concerned that there are more than two million alcoholics among a population of 33 million people. In addition, a recent study made by scholars Down Under indicated that one out of every 20 Australian males over 15 years of age is an alcoholic.

But America may hold the dubious distinction of beating them all.

Dr. Roger Egeberg of the U.S. Department of Health, Education, and Welfare has labeled alcoholism the number one public health problem in the nation. It affects some 9 million Americans directly—as well as an estimated 36 million family members. The National Council on Alcoholism simply calls it the most neglected illness in our society.

Dr. William B. Terhune, a nationally respected alcoholism expert, has warned that if the present trend continues, one out of every eight adult Americans now living will end up as an alcoholic. California officials have claimed that one in five residents will be listed as a problem drinker by 1985 unless the current increase rate is dramatically halted.

Sociologist Walter S. Krusich has pointed to the generally accepted statistical evidence that, if twelve people begin to drink socially together, one will become an alcoholic within ten years and three others will end up with serious drinking problems. "One might point to the fact that eight of the twelve are having no problem," he says. "While this is true, the fact remains that four out of twelve, or one out of three, did have a problem.

"I'm an abstainer," he adds, "first, because I feel the

71

odds are much too short and, secondly, because there is no test which can predetermine which four of the twelve who begin to drink socially will have a problem."

The statisticians may argue among themselves about the actual number of so-called "social drinkers" who will end up needing help for an alcohol problem. But not even the most generous odds should be taken lightly. Krusich uses the widely accepted norm of one in twelve, while other experts settle for one in eighteen. However, it may be that Herman Kregel is closest to the truth when he talks about The Thirteenth American—that one person out of every thirteen who is a largely forgotten and forlorn member of the most affluent society in the world!

What, if anything, is being done about this national scandal?

This is one area where government, drawing upon its financial and personnel resources, has taken a long, hard look at a problem and done something constructive about it. In 1970, for example, President Nixon signed into law the Hughes-Javits-Moss bill, thereby allocating more than $300 million for the prevention of alcoholism and the treatment and rehabilitation of the alcoholic himself. These funds are now being used to combat the disease among federal employees and armed forces personnel. They are also being used to assist state and local agencies concerned with the problem. Other federal funds have been earmarked to the Department of Transportation to identify and then control the drinking driver—and to ram home the fact that alcohol and gasoline don't mix.

One private program which has received financial assistance under the act is the Berkeley Center for Alcohol Studies, headed by Dr. Kregel and located on the beautiful campus of the Pacific School of Religion in Berkeley, California. In addition to offering the nation's only master's degree for clergymen in the field, the center conducts a two-week summer session for chaplains and other clergy working with alcoholics and their families. In 1972, fifty-one ordained men and women attended the summer school under a grant provided by the National Institute of Mental Health and the National Institute on Alcohol Abuse and Alcoholism.

Herman Kregel himself is a jovial Dutch Reformed minister whose knowledge of alcoholism is matched only by his knowledge of the Bible. He'll quote a suitable text spontaneously. For example, when one summer student complained that he didn't feel like changing his bed-sheets, Dr. Kregel shot back: "He that is filthy; let him be filthy still."

But the sharp wit vanishes when Herman Kregel talks about the overwhelming number of pastors and laymen who have demonstrated what he calls "passionate apathy" toward the plight of The Thirteenth American. He believes that clergymen have adopted this stance for three reasons:

One. They don't want to "get burned again" since the great church crusade for prohibition has been repealed.

Two. Many recoil against memories of the day when the only test of Christian piety involved abstinence from beverage alcohol.

Three. Extreme polarization has occurred between those who believe that the only problem is alcohol and those who believe it is not a problem at all.

And, while studies show that 70 percent of those in A.A. first turned to their pastor for help, the fact remains that the churches don't have a very good track record when it comes to racing against John Barleycorn.

There are some evangelical leaders who are candid enough to admit that well-meaning Christians can often do more harm than good by thinking that sobriety will come on the wings of an appropriate Scripture text. One of them is the Rev. Charles T. Knippel, alcoholism expert for The Lutheran Mission Association of Metropolitan St. Louis, who insists that fellow Christians must first seek to understand the alcoholic's defense system and inner experience.

"We need to realize that deep inside the alcoholic feels guilty and bad about himself," Mr. Knippel informed a recent Lutheran Hour audience. "If we approach him in a way that makes him feel worse, he'll probably become angry and turn away."

This Missouri Synod Lutheran churchman suggests that the alcoholic needs to hear more about grace and less about law. "Actually," he says, "the alcoholic is already having a real-life law experience, that is, he is feeling the pain of dealing with life in a way counter to God's design. The way we can be helpful, it seems to me, is by helping the alcoholic to identify the cause of his pain within the terms of his illness and to show him the inappropriate way he is dealing with life. Then we help him know that help is available—medical help, Alcoholics Anonymous, and the Church."

Charles Knippel's approach to the problem recognizes that alcoholism involves the whole man—body, mind and spirit. He does not *condemn* the alcoholic, but neither does he *commend* his deviant behavior.

There is no doubt that Jesus felt very much at home among the winebibbers of His own age (Matthew 11: 19). For He made it indelibly clear: "I am not come to call the righteous, but sinners to repentance" (Matthew 9: 13). He further shocked the spiritually self-satisfied by informing them with a note of scorn that only the sick recognize their need of the Great Physician (9: 12). Our Lord was a Man among men.

However, it is impossible to envision the Master working as a bartender—particularly in our own day when alcoholism has reached epidemic proportions. Therefore, it is just somewhat incongruous to think of a young clergyman who conducts a "ministry of presence" by serving drinks in a bar on New York City's upper east side. It is quite reasonable for a minister to want to carry on a counseling ministry outside the restricted confines of his own parish. At the same time, it is difficult to imagine that very much good can actually be accomplished by this "Good Joe" approach to the sacred calling. While some problem drinkers might be led to seek help by a pastor-bartender, the real "value" of this so-called "ministry" may have been pointed out by the bar owner himself: "He creates a good atmosphere and makes women feel free to come in on their own. A lot of people also think it's fun to have their drinks served by a minister."

If this approach raises serious questions for Christians, the opposite extreme may also be counterproductive. This is the position of so many evangelicals who assume that the only cause of alcoholism is alcohol. What the problem drinker must do, they say, is to put the cork in the bottle and accept Jesus Christ as Savior and Lord.

There is no doubt that countless lives have been radically altered by the transforming power of the Holy Spirit. In other instances, alcoholics have been lost to the Gospel by the rescue mission approach to this problem. Joe Rosenfield, Jr., author of *The Happiest Man in the World,* speaks for many alcoholics when he reveals his own contempt for the "salesmen of salvation" who nightly beckon the unfortunate habitues of skid row to "take a nosedive for Jesus." "I still shudder, and will continue to do so for the rest of my life, whenever I hear the word 'mission,' " he writes. "I learned what it means to have to listen to a psalm-singing (evangelist) preach at you for an hour, while your guts are growling from hunger, your vitals clamoring for a crumb of bread, your stomach starving for soup."

However, many who work with the skid row alcoholic defend what *Time* magazine called the "sing-for-your-supper" approach of rescue mission evangelism. "Christ spoke to 5,000 people all day before He fed them," says Jerry Dunn, president of the International Union of Gospel Missions. "If a man is really hungry we will feed him, but we don't apologize for requiring attendance at worship. If we don't give them a foundation to build their lives on, we give them nothing."

The fact is that Jerry Dunn himself stands in the tradition of other Christian leaders who found freedom from alcohol inside a rescue mission. "I am an alcoholic," he says. "I know what it is like to burn with a desire to drink that is so overpowering that family, job, and friends mean nothing . . . . I also know the joy of deliverance from the power of alcohol addiction." He found his answer in Jesus Christ.

Therefore, it hardly behooves anyone to brush aside the work being done by such dedicated men. In one calendar year, rescue missions across the country served 14 million meals and, as *Time* noted, "usually without any public financial aid and often at a low cost that public institutions would envy." Says psychiatrist David Morley, "The mission's love goes to a segment of humanity that we like to ignore."

However, the rescue mission approach to alcoholism raises some serious questions for evangelicals. For one thing, some studies show that as little as three percent of the nation's alcoholics end up on skid row. The overwhelming majority are like the guy and gal next door— the housewife who hides her bottle in the clothes hamper, or the lawyer or construction worker who manages to keep his job in spite of his problem.

One might also legitimately question Jerry Dunn's observation that Jesus offered the 5,000 salvation before He fed them sandwiches. The fact is that the multitudes who came to hear Him preach were presumably healthy men, women, and children who could afford to miss a meal. If there were any alcoholics in that crowd, it is more likely to assume that the Master got them sober before He offered them that life-giving water that quenches the thirst for booze (John 4: 13, 14). It's pretty hard for a shaking, sweating drunk to think about anything else when he desperately needs another drink.

At any rate, Christians are not the only ones who are divided on this matter of salvaging the lives of the alcoholic and his family. That this problem often is thwarted by more emotion than knowledge was evident at a recent conference called by the University of Michigan. Its sponsors included government agencies, insurance companies, and organizations representing the liquor industry. However, Paul J. C. Friedlander, writing in the *New York Times,* reported that the conference "stumbled into wrangling and its program fell apart midway," when "an ideological brawl (erupted) over how to attack the drunk-driving problem."

Friedlander pointed out that the licensed beverage industry and the insurance companies both had a vested interest in the findings of the conference. The one wanted to promote the proper and safe usage of its products, while the other sought law enforcement and a decrease in accident claims. While the police were critical of court personnel who reduced drunk driving citations to misdemeanors, Friedlander noted, other government agencies appeared to be sheltering alcoholics under "their bureaucratic wing."

Friedlander pointed out that agency representatives correctly labeled alcoholics as sick people. "But," he continued, "they kept insisting that alcoholics require sympathy and care and that strict law enforcement and barring them from highways is somehow unfair." He wrote:

> This caused the big fight at the seminar, because the Department of Transportation (DOT) is spending

millions of tax dollars originating and supporting local programs against drunk driving.

And what happened when the DOT people got back to Washington? They and their advertising agency knuckled under to the Alcohol Abuse people, redid their advertising program to delete suggestions of punitive action against drunk drivers, softened the already soft message.

Meanwhile, whatever the actual facts in this case, thousands annually continue to die in the erratic path of the drinking driver. Thousands more succumb to insanity or death because of alcoholism, while the total human toll can never be pegged only in terms of a $15 billion loss to the nation's economy.

"We have dinned into our ears hour after hour the problems of the Vietnam war," Paulist Father James F. Cunningham told the National Safety Congress in 1970. "Yet we have here a greater war—free from all the complexities of ideology and politics . . . . (There are) no Congressional medals, no Purple Hearts, and no purpose, only a waste of God's precious gift of life. This calls for the application of moral and ethical standards."

Herman Kregel insists that the time is long overdue for the Church to break its "conspiracy of silence."

"What would you think if the astronauts came back with a virus that would kill 1,600 Americans every week?" he asks fellow Christians. "Or if one out of every thirteen bus passengers was killed weekly in highway accidents? Yet alcohol kills a proportionate number each week.

"If a teenager jumped out of a window high on marijuana," he notes, "the story would be on the front pages of every newspaper in the country. But little is said if a youth high on booze is killed wrapping the family car around a tree."

Kregel insists that the churches can serve as a needed catalyst to bring the alcoholic into contact with treatment resources. "Pastors may be the only ones," he says, "who can assume leadership in bringing other leaders of fragmented, competing, jealous agencies together.

"There are not enough psychiatrists in the entire United States to give one hour a week to all of the alcoholics in California alone," he claims. "Besides, they are reported to have one of the poorest records with problem drinkers of any profession in the country.

"A boy Scout with love in his heart," he adds, "can do more for the recovering alcoholic than the most brilliant psychiatrist who hates the guts of the alcoholic."

Like most experts in the field of alcohol addiction, Kregel holds Alcoholics Anonymous in particularly high regard. Its members not only have the highest recovery rate, but A.A. itself hews to the firm policy of cooperating with others in the field without identifying itself with any outside causes. It thereby avoids all public controversies.

But Kregel points out that A.A. admits that it is able to reach only a fraction of those who desperately need help. There are well over a half million A.A. members scattered in 92 countries around the world—about 300,000 of them in the United States. However, some nine million people—every thirteenth American—need help in this country alone!

That the churches have their own vested interest in this gigantic national public health problem was forcefully brought home to one pastor when he recently made what he thought was a routine parish call. Instead the wife met him at the door and said of her husband, "I told him that if he continued drinking, I was going to call you."

The man, a faithful member of the congregation, tried to brush away his wife's concern. "Ah," he said defensively, "I only have a few beers."

However, the minister was himself a recovered alcoholic. At one time, he could con his way to his next drink along with the best of them. So he simply told his good friend his own story. Yet he still was unprepared for the man's admission that he had actually eight bottles of whiskey hidden throughout the house—and away from the watchful eye of his disapproving wife!

"It is clear that problem drinkers are found in every parish, and that age, sex, or social status have little to do with who is or who is not an alcoholic," says the Rev. Samuel B. Bird, chairman of the Committee on Alcoholism of the Episcopal Diocese of New York.

Evangelicals are hiding their heads in the sand if they think problem drinking is confined only to those churches which have a relaxed view about the use of beverage alcohol. There probably isn't a congregation in the United States that doesn't have a problem drinker or families whose lives have been made intolerable by the abuse of alcohol.

The gulf between preaching and practice was clearly evident in a survey conducted some time ago, involving a suburban Kansas City church of 1,700 members, said to represent "a cross section of American Methodism." That study showed that 85 percent of the men and 74 percent of the women did drink on occasion—despite the official stand of their denomination favoring total abstinence. Meanwhile, the Baptists still retain their lead among mainline Protestant churches in the ratio between occasional drinkers and abstainers. But one recent survey indicated that 48 percent of the American Baptists are not averse to having a social drink.

Moreover, problem drinking is not confined to the comfortable pew. It often hits the man behind the pulpit as well. In 1966, for example, *Newsweek* magazine reported that Roman Catholic officials were concerned about the estimated four thousand "whiskey priests" serving in dioceses across the country.

The number of Protestant clergy afflicted by the disease has never been documented. However, many denominational executives have had the unhappy task of having to deal with the ordained problem drinker, often at the insistence of a disillusioned congregation. While the clergyman-alcoholic generally gets the "kid glove treatment" when his problem is first discovered, there often comes the time when prudence dictates that the individual must be sacrificed for the institution. In one instance, a once promising Ph.D candidate ended up as a dishwasher before continuing the downward path to the Bowery. Christians may talk a lot about salvation—but they generally offer little hope to the prodigal shepherd or his family.

Statistically, however, alcohol may take an even higher toll in other professions. For example, the New York *Medical Journal* recently observed that "a tragic number" of doctors, dentists, nurses, psychologists, and pharmacists have serious drinking problems. Unfortunately, said the *Journal,* "the (medical) profession itself, in an endeavor to protect its image, creates the protective device behind which the individual may hide, and even perish."

Dr. Matthew Ross, professor of psychiatry at the University of Rhode Island, told the Fifth World Congress of Psychiatry that the suicide rate among doctors is double that for all white Americans. He reported that alcoholism is associated with forty percent of these deaths, and that the depressed physician, fearing further loss of self-esteem, may compound his problem by self-medication.

A recent national survey made by the Controller General estimated that ninety-five percent of the alcoholics in the United States are employable, family-centered, individuals. One in three is a woman.

The report showed that about fifty percent of the nation's problem drinkers have attended or graduated from college, while an additional thirty-seven percent attended high school. Thirty percent were manual laborers, twenty-five percent, white-collar workers—and forty-five percent were in the professional or managerial class. Less than five percent end up on skid row.

"Though the word 'alcoholic' sometimes brings to mind a reeling, rheumy-eyed derelict," says Gerald M. Knox, "few alcoholics actually fit the description . . . . As a group, they're indistinguishable, representing both sexes, a variety of ages, and every race, creed, and calling. As individuals, most of them meet the criteria of middle-class America; they're married, have nice homes, raise a couple of kids or more, live with their families, and go to work or keep house."

Three physicians associated with the Silver Hill Foundation, a private psychiatric hospital in New Canaan, Connecticut, told the seventeenth annual meeting of the Academy of Psychosomatic Medicine that the plight of upper-class alcoholism has been largely neglected in research. No longer a "plague of the poor," the trio noted, "it is precisely the hazard of wealth and power, and the fact that these individuals can take care of themselves so well, that their illness can be concealed until the individual patient may in certain instances no longer be amenable to treatment." It is a well-established fact that the older the problem drinker gets, the harder it is to help him.

Some studies indicate that there are about two million women alcoholics. But this figure may represent only the tip of the iceberg, since women generally do a better job of hiding their problem. In fact, some experts claim that the incidence of alcoholism may well be just as high among women as it is among men. However, says Gerald Knox, "intensified efforts to protect female problem drinkers against exposure lowers the probability of detection. Also, men usually feel less need, and have less opportunity, to drink unobserved, making it more difficult for them to keep alcohol addiction a secret."

Consequently, a great conspiracy develops to "protect" the woman alcoholic from exposure. Housewives have the built-in "advantage" of not having to face a suspicious boss or fellow employees. Husbands often do little more than threaten their wives, or throw up their hands in resignation, when they find a sodden spouse or a secret supply carefully hidden in the bathroom water closet, a garbage pail, or underneath a mattress—occasionally on the husband's side of the bed! The family doctor often becomes the unwitting co-conspirator by being conned into treating the patient for anything other than alcoholism. Yet the experts are unanimous that the kindest thing that can be done is to confront the alcoholic with the problem in an understanding, nonjudgmental manner. Let him know there is hope. His life may well depend upon it.

This goes for the thousands of men and women who have been described as "half alcoholics." Alcoholics Anonymous calls them "periodics" in contrast to the daily drinker. They may be sober for months, and then go off on a two-week drunk. Or they may drink themselves into semiconsciousness every weekend. "In many ways," says Los Angeles psychiatrist Carl Marusak, "these men and women may be as sick as the alcoholic who drinks himself into the hospital or doctor's office . . . . People should live a complete life. These people are living only marginally."

However, if anything should shake the Church out of its lethargy, it is the alarming fact that between thirty to forty percent of America's teenagers drink excessively —and the majority of them will wind up as alcoholics. Moreover, Graham Finney, head of New York City's Addiction Services Agency, recently reported one study showed ninety percent of the teenagers in treatment for heroin addiction started with alcohol.

If this figure sounds sensational, Joe Feurey of the New York *Post* can point to several other studies which also show a correlation between alcohol and narcotics addiction. For example, the President's Commission on

Marijuana and Drug Abuse concluded that alcoholism was more prevalent than pot-smoking among heroin addicts. "And," says Feurey, "a recent study by the Health Insurance Institute indicated that alcohol had led to heroin addiction in certain individuals. In the study, ninety-three percent of the addicts had been drinkers. Twenty-four percent were considered social drinkers. Sixty-nine percent were found to be 'alcohol abusers.'"

However, the most sobering thought for parents and teachers to ponder involves the rise of cross-addiction. The Health Services Administration of New York City has found that increasing numbers of narcotics addicts are becoming cross-addicted to alcohol, while increasing numbers of alcoholics are becoming also addicted to other drugs. The HSA has therefore concluded that once an individual has obtained a mood change through alcohol, he or she is likely to use other drugs interchangeably.

Actress Mercedes McCambridge, herself a recovered alcoholic, has said flatly: "Drug addicts are measured by thousands. Alcoholics are measured by the millions." However, New York City spends forty times as much money on the treatment of narcotics addiction as it does on the treatment of alcoholism—even though the death rate for problem drinkers in the city is six times as high as that of hard-core drug users.

A recent Foley college poll taken on 100 campuses across the country showed that, by almost three to one, students rate marijuana better for your health than liquor. However, the pollsters noted, "religious beliefs and backgrounds play an important role in student attitudes. Catholics and Protestants portray a much more conservative attitude toward marijuana. Seventy-three percent of the Catholics and sixty-six percent of the Protestants rated liquor as better at a party." In some instances, the survey indicated, "alcoholic beverage use, especially wines, appears to complement use of marijuana."

One recent development among youth involves the use of "pop wines," which grossed $190 million for producers in 1971. By 1975, trade sources predict that sales will zoom to 30 million cases or more—a total, says Jane Leek of the *Los Angeles Times,* which is being "skillfully nurtured by an industry focusing straight at the young."

The widespread use of alcoholic beverages by teenagers has made some state officials have second thoughts about lowering the legal age for drinking from twenty-one to eighteen. For example, *U.S. News & World Report* noted a "shocking rise" of 110 percent in the number of highway accidents involving teenagers in a six-month period after Michigan lowered the legal drinking age. In Tennessee, Major George Currey, commander of the youth-guidance division of the Nashville Police Department, considers the enfranchisement of young drinkers "a drastic mistake." "They lowered the age by three years," he says, "so now we have fifteen-year-olds slipping around getting drinks purchased by eighteen-year-olds they associate with.

"I'm afraid," Major Currey adds, "we were so worried about getting their votes we forgot about their physical and moral well-being."

Studies have shown that kids get "turned off" by any scare campaigns directed toward curbing their behavior. Yet the fact remains that there is a direct correlation between the use of alcohol and sexual indiscretions which can mar a young person for life. For example, one survey among residents of a home for unmarried mothers showed that seventy-nine percent had been drinking when they became pregnant. Another sampling of 7,000 broken marriages listed the most common cause for divorce— twenty-nine percent of the cases—as "excessive drinking."

Meanwhile, the rise of venereal disease is reaching

epidemic proportions in the United States and elsewhere in the world. In Poland, according to the Associated Press, doctors regard alcohol as "a prime cause" for the upswing. "Statistics indicate," says AP, "that three-fifths of Warsaw residents contracting a venereal disease were drunk at the time."

The Surgeon General's report on smoking indicates that the scare techniques are also of limited value among adults. But those who enjoy "bending the elbow" should pause and consider these facts before they pick up that next drink:

. . . Several studies have shown that alcoholics run a greater risk of suffering from a slowly deteriorating heart disease.

. . . While alcohol itself is not believed to be a carcinogen, it is "associated" with liver cancer, cancer of the pancreas, oral cancer, cancer of the larynx, the esophagus, the rectum—and, says Bernard Glemser, "with cancer of *any part* of the gastrointestinal tract and the associated organs of the digestive system."

Meanwhile, New York City Fire Commissioner Robert O. Lowery, commenting on 299 deaths in a total of 125,000 fires in the city in 1971, had this to say: "The largest single cause of fatal fires is the combination of smoking and drowsiness. If you add the factor of intoxication . . . you have the cause of more than forty percent of all fatal fires."

Psychologist Henry Wechsler, a research director of the Medical Foundation of Boston, adds this note: "Twenty percent of all accidental deaths occur in the home, where it has been estimated that two thirds of all alcohol is consumed." During a one-year period, twenty-two percent of the 620 home accident cases treated at Massachusetts General Hospital had positive Breathalyzer readings at the time of admission.

Other grim news accounts have reported that half of

the 500 carbon monoxide victims who died in their cars in one year had been sleeping off a drunk . . . that two American servicemen died in Pleiku, South Vietnam, after "playing chicken" with a live hand grenade during a heavy drinking bout . . . that Soviet officials are alarmed by the relationship between booze and drownings in the Moscow area.

Heavy drinkers are mighty poor risks for life insurance companies!

However, Maurice Blond, general agent for Travelers Insurance Company in New York City, has indicated that an alcoholic stands a pretty good chance of getting coverage without premium penalties—provided he is getting professional help for his problem.

Alcohol has ravaged the lives of untold millions of American families. Nowhere is the tragedy more evident than in the number of shattered dreams, wrecked ambitions and soiled reputations.

One team of psychiatrists who studied the personality traits of scores of bad-check artists discovered that about half of them admitted "the money obtained was used for the purchase of alcohol, with a third claiming they were drinking at the time of the offense."

In one instance, a respected scholar at the State University of New York was convicted of misappropriating funds from a research grant. The court showed leniency when it learned the man had a serious drinking problem. But it remains to be seen whether the academic community will demonstrate similar compassion when he attempts to reenter the already tight university job market.

However, the most unusual case may be that of an employee of a Tulsa armored car service who walked off the job with close to $134,000, part of which he blew during a three-week spree in Los Angeles. He then flew back to Tulsa, returned about $121,000 to his employer and surrendered to authorities. The court let him off with a five-year suspended sentence after he agreed to repay the cost of his binge.

But his troubles were far from over. The Internal Revenue Service stepped into the act and said that he would have to declare the entire amount of his embezzlement as earned income the year he took the funds. It demanded $73,265 in taxes.

"Embezzled funds generally are considered taxable income," explained the *Wall Street Journal*. "But under some circumstances embezzlers have escaped taxes. A few months ago (early 1972) the Tax Court ruled that money a man embezzled could be treated as a loan rather than income because the same year he took it he signed a pledge to repay it. But in (this) case, the Tax Court backed the IRS.

"The court stated that (the defendant) hadn't made repayment arrangements until the year after he took the money," the *Journal* reported. "It also rejected his contention that he hadn't 'received unrestricted use of the money' in the few remaining days of the year he took it because of 'excessive use of alcohol.' "

Stranger yet is the tale of a career serviceman who was arrested on charges of conspiring to transfer secret documents to a foreign power in exchange for a verbal assurance that the recipient government would bring pressure to end the Vietnam War. The officers at his court martial were not impressed when he stated he hatched his incredible plot in an alcoholic stupor.

Another man threatened to hijack an airliner if he wasn't served six more drinks by the stewardess. He got off a lot easier than the serviceman. But he was sternly informed by a federal judge in Omaha that he must abstain from liquor for at least a year—and join Alcoholics Anonymous.

This is what alcohol can do to otherwise respectable people. Yet the Licensed Beverage Industries still promotes the illusion: "One American custom that has never changed: a friendly social drink."

Of course, the distillers warn that "the hostess who pours the mostest is a poor hostess." They also advise motorists to know their limits if they are going to drink and drive. "If you choose to drink," they say, "drink responsibly."

But what about that Thirteenth American who has crossed that invisible line between controlled and uncontrolled drinking? Does anyone honestly think that such pious pronouncements help either him or his family?

Moreover, if it is true that about ten percent of the drinking public consumes about eighty percent of the alcoholic beverages produced, then the question arises as to whether the liquor industry could survive without the regular business of the problem drinker.

But no one likes a drunk, the distillers least of all. For he gives their product and the industry a mighty poor public relations image.

While the LBI promotes the fact that it has spent large sums for research into the causes of alcoholism, Herman Kregel has noted that it has supported government resistance to plans to allocate a portion of the $8 billion collected nationally each year in liquor taxes to aid the industry's "best customers."

"I say rather facetiously," says Kregel, "that the only guy who really gets gypped in this country . . . is the alcoholic. These are the ones, as they near the end of the road, who aren't even getting any insurance or social security or anything like that on their previous investments."

There are still those who think that alcoholism is a laughing matter. One agency called Rent-a-Drunk will provide an actor feigning inebriation to liven up your party. But for some reason there are millions of deprived families across America who can't seem to get the point of the joke. For them alcoholism isn't funny. It's a disaster.

But the moralists aren't doing much either to help the situation. They still insist that the alcoholic is a drunken bum who could help himself if he only used a little willpower. One is reminded of the wife who chided her husband for not going to church to get help for his drinking problem. "But, honey," he remarked, "the bar is so warm and the church is so cold." A lot of alcoholics would echo his words with a loud Amen!

Yet the biggest stumbling block to recovery comes not from the Christian community but from people who tolerate drunken behavior and apply social pressures upon the alcoholic to have a "sociable drink." Says Dr. Kregel: "To respect the right of someone not to drink in our cocktail-oriented society is more needed than the existing attitudes about everyone's right or need to drink."

Arnold S. Linsky, a University of New Hampshire sociologist, has concluded that American attitudes toward the problem drinker are changing. He notes that traditional attitudes favoring religion, willpower and legal restraints are beginning to lose favor in the public mind as more people recognize alcoholism as a medical-psychological problem.

Linsky's findings, published in the *Quarterly Journal of Studies on Alcohol,* led him to speculate that the understanding and sympathy now being extended toward alcoholics may be a consequence of the "gradual widening and institutionalizing of compassion."

Let's hope he's right because America is now being swept by an Andromeda Strain more deadly than addiction to other drugs. We don't need any virus from outer space to further foul the nation's environment. Alcohol is already killing and maiming our people by the millions.

And most people just don't seem to care!

5

Demon or Disease?

> *"Woe unto them that rise up early in the morning, that they may follow strong drink; that continue until night, till wine inflame them . . . Therefore my people are gone into captivity, because they have no knowledge: and their honourable men are famished, and their multitude dried up with thirst"* (Isaiah 5: 11, 13).

Marxist President Salvador Allende of Chile has one thing in common with many conservative American Christians.

Both think alcoholics are bums!

Allende has threatened to publish the names of absentee workers who take time off their jobs to nurse hangovers and other symptoms connected with problem drinking. "I am going to denounce those alcoholics and bums before the entire country," he warned. "We have to appeal to the conscience, using persuasion and dialogue, to show the workers their obligations. That is what we are doing."

President Allende's caustic attitude toward the problem drinker is quite significant because he is a physician as well as a politician. Like many who favor prohibition in

91

the United States, he rejects the disease concept of alcoholism out-of-hand. He would agree with those who claim that only alcohol can make an alcoholic.

In all fairness to those who work for national prohibition, the most reliable statistical evidence completely demolished the claim that drinking increased in America following enactment of the Volsted Act more than a half century ago. In fact, statistics compiled by both the Berkeley and Rutgers schools of alcohol studies show a marked decrease in the national consumption of beverage alcohol during Prohibition. Ironically, however, other statistics indicate that problem drinking was on the rise throughout the period.

The complexities involved in drafting a workable national policy on the use and abuse of alcohol have been suggested by Walter Krusich, who raises serious questions about the so-called disease concept. On the one hand, he notes a higher standard of living in "dry" areas, such as Gujarat State in India, where prohibition has been in effect since 1947. He also argues, quite justifiably, "there isn't a country in the world that can say, 'We drink in moderation and have no problems.' " On the other hand, Mr. Krusich believes that prohibition is practical only in a situation in which at least seventy to eighty percent of the people are solidly behind the concept. "To legislate prohibition," he says, "where the great majority of the people do not want it and where the officials, therefore, would not enforce it, would probably produce a chaotic situation."

Moreover, a study reported in the *Quarterly Journal of Alcohol Studies* shows a correlation between problem drinking and conflict concerning the matter. For example, that study indicated that the chances are 50-50 that a person will use alcohol destructively to solve his own problems if he comes from a home in which alcohol was abused. However, the chances are two in three that the same thing will happen to the drinker who comes from a home in which alcohol was considered the Devil's Brew or the "forbidden fruit." In both cases, says Dr. Cheatham, the individual did not know *how to drink* in a saturated society!

The problem is compounded for Christians who take their Bibles seriously. For only the person who rejects the authority of Scripture can deny a uniform judgment of God from Genesis to Revelation against the person who misuses beverage alcohol.

Both Biblical and Talmudic Judaism have traditionally imposed strong strictures against those who drink excessively. The Jewish attitude has been that only Gentiles become drunkards. However, the Jewish community has now come to the point where it must deal with the rising incidence of alcoholism among its members as both Jewish and Christian values are threatened by a growing and pervasive secularism.

The Mosaic Law decreed that the drunkard should be stoned to death so that this "evil [might be put] away from among you; and all Israel shall hear, and fear" (Deuteronomy 21: 21). The writer of Proverbs also condemned the excessive use of alcohol, because "at the last it biteth like a serpent, and stingeth like an adder" (23: 32). He further warned that the drunkard would know poverty, contentions, and foolish babbling (23: 21, 29, 30). "Wine is a mocker," he wrote, "strong drink is raging: and whosoever is deceived thereby is not wise" (20: 1).

The Old Testament prophets were particularly hard on those who abused the use of alcohol. They warned that excessive drinking could only lead to personal and national humiliation. Yet these divinely inspired observers of their times have left us with a profile of the alcoholic which is as up-to-date as the latest clinical study!

Isaiah spoke of loss of control and the morning drink,

both of which are symptomatic of incipient alcoholism (5: 11). He also hinted that problem drinkers were even then turning to mixed drinks in an effort to get a bigger charge (5: 22). Joel pointed to the utter loss of self-respect (3: 3), and to the dilemma of the alcoholic who desperately needs a drink and can't get one (1: 5). Amos suggested that the downward path leads the problem drinker to abandon his own standards and to associate with those whose moral values are questionable (6: 6). But it was Hosea who showed the abject hopelessness of the alcoholic when he declared that "wine and new wine take away the heart" (4: 11).

However, the prophets were no less severe in their denunciation of those who push alcoholic drinks on their guests. These great moral leaders of Israel singled out those who sought to ensnare their prophets and priests by offering them beverages which would cause them to "err in vision . . . [and] stumble in judgment" (Isaiah 28: 7; Amos 2: 12; Micah 2: 11). Yet it was Habakkuk (2: 15) who summed up the prophets' scorn for those hosts who insist on plying their guest with alcohol: "Woe unto him that giveth his neighbour drink, that puttest thy bottle to him, and makest him drunken also."

The New Testament writers have a shock in store for those who would argue that excessive drinking is more easily accommodated under grace than under law. Our Lord warned His followers to be on guard against drunkenness lest His return take them by surprise (Luke 21: 34). Paul categorically declared that drunkards would not inherit the Kingdom of God (Galatians 5: 21; I Corinthians 6: 10). He even went so far as to admonish the saints at Corinth not to sit at the same table with a brother who used alcohol in excess (I Corinthians 5: 11).

There are sound theological and therapeutic principles behind this "intolerant" Biblical position. For one thing, the alcoholic has abandoned any faith he may have had in the God of the Bible. His only god is the bottle; and the sooner he becomes aware of the true character of this deceptive deity, the sooner he will come to his senses and flee the far country and return home to the waiting Father.

Christians should not apologize for their "blue nose" attitude toward excessive drinking if their ultimate goal is the salvation of the alcoholic. They may well take stock of their own spiritual condition if they are filled with self-righteous pride in the presence of a hopeless drunk (Luke 18: 9-14). But those who boast of their tolerance toward man's indiscretions might also question their own motives. For blatant hypocrisy so often lies at the root of their feelings. They will excuse alcoholic behavior—up to a point. But then they drop the problem drinker like a hot potato when he becomes obnoxious or asks for money for another drink. What's more, such "liberals" often condone their own drinking habits in light of a brother's excess. Someone has sagely defined the alcoholic as the man "who drinks more than I do."

Nothing is so cruel as allowing the alcoholic to evade his real problem. He needs to be drawn up short and forced to see that booze—and nothing else—is the source of all of his troubles. At the same time, he needs to learn that normal frustrations and pain are part of the maturing process. As Upton Sinclair put it: "Not drinking is no easy passport to happiness, no automatic assurance of a good and happy and creative life. What it *does* do is to increase the odds enormously."

No one has better illustrated the demonic aspect of alcoholism than Mr. Sinclair, the son of a liquor salesman who was unable to resist his own wares. As a result of his father's tragic battle with the bottle, this great American author was a lifelong teetotaler. His personal hatred for booze eventually led him to write the bone-chilling book, *The Cup of Fury,* in which he reveals how alcohol completely demoralized and then destroyed so many of his distinguished friends—Jack London, Dylan Thomas, Sinclair Lewis, O. Henry, Stephen Crane, and Eugene V. Debs.

Even more distressing is Upton Sinclair's tale of how the smart set repeatedly tried to get him to take "a sociable drink." H. L. Mencken was bound and determined to turn him into a drunkard. But Sinclair holds the bulk of his fury for those who would stoop so low as to slip alcohol into the glass of an unsuspecting problem drinker, who was valiantly seeking to remain sober.

If anything should make Christians maintain their integrity regarding the misuse of alcohol, it is this lucid polemic against John Barleycorn. Christians may reject aberrant alcoholic behavior; but seldom do they reject the alcoholic himself. Such is not the case with the world. There are thousands of recovering alcoholics who will gladly testify that they were welcome at the neighborhood bar only so long as they had the price of the next drink. But perhaps one of the most pitiful examples of the world's cruelty is revealed in Sinclair's tragic tale of a great publisher who flirted with the bottle and died broke and full of debts. Only six erstwhile drinking friends showed up at his funeral, even though he had helped to launch so many literary careers. The sad fact is that no one likes a drunk, the world least of all!

Moreover, it just might be possible that the Bible's condemnation of excessive drinking is reserved not so much for the alcoholic as for that sophisticated and worldly-wise individual who boasts that he "can drink like a man." For example, Isaiah's judgment against the abuse of beverage alcohol is set in the context of those who "call evil good, and good evil" (5: 20). He lashes out as much against corrupt realtors (5: 8-10) and sensual materialists (5: 12) as he does against that man who follows after strong drink. There is ample Biblical support to believe that God is able and willing to help the *tragically sick;* but even He cannot do anything for the *boastful sinner* (Luke 5: 27-35).

Each Christian must come to terms with alcohol and alcoholism in light of the Bible. Some may conclude on purely practical grounds that the risks are too great to imbibe in an occasional drink. Others may refrain because they do not want to be a party to causing a weaker brother to stumble (Romans 14: 13-21). Still others may follow the course of Luther, Calvin, and Knox and support moderation over total abstinence. While these great Reformers all condemned drunkenness, one of them once remarked facetiously: "If someone thinks you are an Anabaptist, go drink a little beer and show him that you are not."

Whatever course the Christian may follow, there is no place for personal pride or for twisting Scripture to conform to one's own convictions on this matter. The Jewish community has always looked upon wine as a gift of God and used it sacramentally. In fact, in the very passage in which Isaiah condemns drunkenness in the strongest terms, he also uses the illustration of Israel being the Lord's vineyard—one that put forth "wild grapes" (5: 1-7).

Jesus and His disciples appear to have used wine in this sacramental way as they sat together in that Upper Room just before He offered Himself up as the Lamb without blemish and without spot. It was in that room that our Lord instituted the Holy Feast of the New Covenant, even as He drank of the wine of the traditional Passover seder (Mark 14: 22-25). However, no such exalted event led Paul to admonish his young friend Timothy to skip that germ-infested water and to "use a little wine for thy stomach's sake and thine often infirmities" (I Timothy 5: 23). Modern tourists to the Near East can tell you that the apostle wasn't talking about soda pop. But neither was he talking about a ninety proof martini or manhattan!

Neither abstinence nor moderation are the final test of Christian piety. We all are rather called to try to speak the truth in love (Ephesians 4: 15).

This Biblical precept is much easier to recite than to follow when it comes to problem drinking. The person who was brutalized as a child by a drunken father might well conclude that excessive tippling is sinful, whereas the recovering alcoholic himself might claim that he was the helpless victim of a terrifying sickness.

Here again the Bible offers some light on the question. There was one occasion when Jesus healed a man who was born blind. When His disciples asked whether the handicap was the result of his sin or that of his parents, the Lord declared that neither were sinners. His blindness rather offered the opportunity for Jesus to manifest "the works of God" (John 9: 1-3). There is not always a correlation between sickness and sin.

But the reverse is also true. There are many illustrations in the New Testament healing narratives in which sickness and sin go hand-in-glove. While modern medicine recognizes that a man's spiritual and emotional condition can undermine his physical well-being, the Pharisees repeatedly opposed Jesus for claiming to forgive sins even as He brought healing to a diseased or disabled body. "Whether is easier, to say," He asked, "Thy sins be forgiven thee; or to say, Arise, and walk?" (Matthew 9: 1-7).

This Biblical principle should have direct bearing upon how Christians approach the extremely complex causes of alcoholism.

Alcoholics Anonymous has traditionally looked upon problem drinking as a three-fold disease, which affects the whole body, mind, and spirit of man. Both the American and British medical associations, as well as the World

Health Organization, tend to agree with this position. In addition, the federal government has now decreed that alcoholics in the armed forces and in federal agencies are sick people in need of sophisticated medical treatment.

Many Christians find this hard to believe. They would agree with Dr. Jules Masserman of Northwestern University, and Dr. Harold A. Mulford of the University of Iowa, both of whom share a minority position that alcoholism is not a disease—but a form of deviant behavior, not unlike excessive eating, sleeping, smoking, gambling or lechery.

"On the basis of a third of a century of intensive interest, laboratory research, and clinical experience in the field," says Dr. Masserman, "I feel justified in maintaining that no one has demonstrated any consistent genetic, constitutional, dietary, infectious, or other purely physiological causes of alcoholism."

However, Dr. Masserman does concede that the excessive intake of any drug can injure body and brain tissue and impair resistance.

The question is: What comes first, the chicken or the egg?

This is a problem which has baffled those in the field of alcoholism research for many years. For example, Dr. Leon A. Greenberg of Yale University, once warned overzealous colleagues not to seek a simplistic solution to alcoholism in either a vitamin deficiency or in the improper functioning of the adrenal glands. Referring to the chicken and egg metaphor in more erudite terms, Dr. Greenberg wrote: "Both of these hypotheses are examples of the classic error in reasoning—*post hoc, ergo propter hoc* —alcoholics suffer vitamin deficiency and adrenal malfunction, therefore the latter are the cause of alcoholism . . . What these hypotheses lack in reality, they seem to make up in simplicity."

Edward J. McGoldrick, Jr., founder and director of

Bridge House in New York City, is an expert in alcoholism rehabilitation who attacks the disease concept on another score. He writes:

If alcoholics are to have any hope of recovery, they must face the truth about themselves, and an essential part of that truth is that they are not sick people, in the physician's sense of the term. The dogma that the cause of the alcoholic's drinking is a disease, though originally promulgated by well-meaning persons, is one of the most pernicious of the widespread misconceptions shrouding the question of who and what is the alcoholic. It received impetus at first from the praiseworthy desire of those interested in helping the alcoholic combat the prejudice of people who felt him beyond redemption or help. It has been happily and joyously embraced by alcoholics the world over as a sanctioned excuse for their excessive drinking. Not only has it proven to be one of the greatest blunders in the field of public relations but also one of the greatest obstacles in the path of the alcoholic's recovery and cure (sic).

To support his contention, McGoldrick quotes Dr. Harry M. Tiebout, long-time booster of A.A. and one of the most knowledgeable psychiatrists in the field. "Actually," wrote Tiebout in *The Grapevine,* "the idea that alcoholism is a disease was reached empirically by pure inferences. It had never been really proved nor does there seem to be much disposition to validate the concept or to round out the picture."

There is no doubt that some alcoholics have used the disease concept to lament their "hopeless" condition and to rationalize themselves into another binge. But there are countless others who have discovered through this concept that they are not crazy or necessarily more immoral than a lot of teetotalers who go on sinning as sober as a judge. For them, the hypothesis offered a way out by demonstrating that they were victims of a treatable, if incurable, illness that could lead to insanity or death.

If the disease concept is a "pernicious" misconception, the demonic illusion that alcoholics might someday return to normal drinking is doubly so. Yet many problem drinkers curse the day when they were led astray by isolated studies which seemed to indicate that some alcoholics might be able to drink socially after extensive therapy.

Dr. Arthur H. Cain, a New York psychologist, holds the dubious distinction of being one of the leading exponents of this often tragic notion. Cain wrote a book, *The Cured Alcoholic,* in which he cited the findings of two University of Michigan researchers, Melvin L. Selzer and William Holloway, who came up with the startling report that thirteen confirmed alcoholics had become social drinkers. He further noted that Dr. D. L. Davies reported that seven problem drinkers were able to drink normally after treatment at Maudsley Hospital in London.

Cain contended that he himself had treated more than fifty alcoholics who no longer need to attend meetings or receive treatment. "Most important," he said, "over twenty of my patients have learned to drink normally, to use alcohol as a beverage, not a psychological crutch.

"There is no scientific evidence that alcoholism is an incurable, physical disease," he continued. "According to current evidence, the origin of uncontrolled drinking is psychological. A person drinks to ease anxiety, depression, boredom, guilt, timidity, inarticulateness. An alcoholic *learns* to become one; he is not born that way. This means that many alcoholics can return to normal drinking without fear of ending up on skid row."

The reaction to these unorthodox claims came swiftly and forcefully from the scientific community. Dr. Tiebout felt obliged to point out that the Maudsley findings in no way ruled out the compulsive element in alcohol addiction. "The statistic that eighty-six out of ninety-three (alcoholics in the study) did not try to reestablish a controlled type of drinking is also significant," he observed.

"For them, irreversibility is still very real and, I suspect, rightfully so. At least they seem to have no intention of making themselves guinea pigs after seven to eleven years of sobriety."

A few years elapsed between the publication of the Davies' findings and the publication of an outstanding book, *Understanding Alcoholism,* compiled and edited by the Christopher D. Smithers Foundation, a leader in the field of alcoholism education. In that book, the editors cite several case studies to illustrate what they call 'the perils of controlled drinking." The last case history is that of Alice who interrupted a pattern of six years of sobriety to have a fling at "controlled drinking." "Alice M. . . . never had a chance to retrace her steps," the chapter ends poignantly. "The progression of the disease, the obsession for alcohol *created by this progression,* and her trust in controlled drinking—all combined to distort what little judgment and sense of survival remained."

As some alcoholics were retracing their steps to hell, they probably never knew that Arthur Cain himself had warned that problem drinkers should not play with fire and touch alcohol again until they had undergone extensive and prolonged therapy. And as cutting as he was of his criticism of A.A., Cain had to concede that A.A. "has been more successful than all other forces in aiding alcoholics to get sober and stay sober."

Meanwhile, Dr. Davies and Dr. Selzer were having some second thoughts about their research. Dr. Davies admitted that "all patients should be advised to aim at total abstinence," while Dr. Selzer suggested that alcoholism may involve more than one single disease entity. "Evidently," he observed, "some alcoholics are left permanently sensitized to alcohol—others are not." He warned that most problem drinkers "are vulnerable for life and, at present, we are unable to predict who will lose the pathological craving and who will not."

Such concessions caused Dr. Marvin A. Block, former chairman of the American Medical Association's Committee on Alcoholism, to declare: "The percentage of failure in those who try to drink again is so overwhelming that those who can return to normal drinking can be discounted statistically as very rare phenomena."

Yet it was left to Dr. Selden Bacon, distinguished director of the Rutgers Center of Alcoholic Studies, to have the last word on the matter. "Alcoholics," he said flatly, "do not drink."

Therefore, Christians who choke on the disease concept of alcoholism should have some second thoughts of their own. Admittedly, there is always the possibility that earthly sobriety will be confused with eternal salvation. There is the further danger that the alcoholic will use the concept to excuse his own excessive drinking while a permissive society excuses his aberrant behavior.

However, the Church has had a pretty dismal record in the reclamation of drunks. And by aligning herself with the forces which reject the disease concept, she finds herself cast among many who argue for "controlled drinking" rather than abstinence. In a word, alcoholism makes some very strange bedfellows!

The Rev. Lyman Beecher, a pioneer of the American Temperance Movement, is reported to have remarked at the bedside of a dying alcoholic: "I indulge the hope that God saw it was a constitutional infirmity, like any other disease."

Dr. E. M. Jellinek, author of *The Disease Concept of Alcoholism* and one of the greatest figures in alcoholism research until his death in 1963, made the observation that both scientists and representatives of the temperance movement were spurred by earlier claims that chronic drunkenness bore the earmarks of an illness.

Dr. Thomas Trotter, a physician in the British Navy, is generally credited as being the first modern investigator to suggest the disease concept. In 1804, Trotter wrote: "In medical language, I consider drunkenness, strictly speaking, to be a disease; produced by a remote cause, giving birth to actions and movements in a living body, that disorder the functions of health . . . . It is to be remembered that a bodily infirmity is not the only thing to be corrected. The habit of drunkenness is a disease of the mind."

Trotter was impressed by the fact that an alcoholic would abandon all worthy pursuits to get that next drink. "The cravings of appetite for the poisonous draught," he noted, "are to the intemperate as much the inclinations of nature, for the time, as a draught of cold water to a traveler panting with thirst in the desert."

Trotter's conclusion was shared on this side of the Atlantic by Dr. Benjamin Rush, physician-general to the Colonial Army during the Revolutionary War and a signatory to the Declaration of Independence. In 1784, Dr. Rush published his own "Inquiry Into the Effects of Ardent Spirits on the Human Body and Mind."

Yet a full century and a half elapsed before the so-called "new approach to alcoholism" received impetus with the establishment of the Center of Alcohol Studies at Yale University (1930), Alcoholics Anonymous (1935), and the National Council on Alcoholism (1944). These three independent forces have remained united in the belief that alcoholism is a disease—not a disgrace.

However, it must be admitted that more than thirty years of exhaustive research has failed to uncover the elusive cause(s) of chronic drunkenness. Some experts retain the belief that alcoholism is a disease entity, while others suggest that it is a symptom of a disease.

Mark Keller, editor of the *Quarterly Journal of Studies on Alcohol,* has noted that scientists probing for physiological causes have tended to attribute the disease to "a biochemical defect of one kind or another which provokes an uncontrollable craving for alcohol." On the other hand, says Keller, "a psychologically-oriented school considers alcoholism to be a manifestation of neurosis based on deficient or arrested development of personality, rooted in childhood. A constitutional predisposition, either to psychic deviation or to alcohol tolerance, is often assumed."

While all of this research has provided invaluable insights in the treatment of alcoholism, there is general agreement today that the alcoholic himself does not fit into any neat stereotype. Few experts are talking any longer about an "alcoholic personality," for example, because personality traits observed in many alcoholics are equally as evident in the general population.

Public confusion regarding the nature of the disease has been heightened by the multiplicity of theories put forth by the experts themselves. It was this problem which led Dr. Jellinek to suggest that alcoholism may be compared to botany. "After looking over the whole world," he said, "I am convinced that alcoholism is a genus, not a species . . . Everyone knows the hibiscus flower—there are over two hundred species. As to genus, *hibiscus* comprises herbs, shrubs and trees. The botanist will ask: Which hibiscus are you referring to? So alcoholism can be considered: Which alcoholism are you talking about? Some may be disease, some may be symptoms of a disease, others may be neither diseases nor symptoms but habits."

However, there is general agreement among scholars that the alcoholic differs from the heavy drinker. "Many authorities feel two main distinctions can be made between heavy drinking and alcoholic drinking," says Gerald Knox. "First, the alcoholic builds up a tolerance to alcohol, which means that his capacity for alcohol increases and it constantly takes more alcohol to have an effect on him. In the heavy drinker, the same amount of alcohol generally produces the same effect: if he drinks more than he usually does, he is affected more. Second, someone who is a heavy drinker and not alcoholic can choose where, when, how much, and with whom he drinks; he can drink or not, as he likes. In short, he has control over his drinking. With the alcoholic, it's the other way around."

But, as Knox points out, some experts believe that such definitions miss the mark. For example, Dr. Morris E. Chafetz, director of the new National Institute on Alcohol Abuse and Alcoholism, has declared: "Alcohol abuse, in one sense, is present any time a person becomes drunk. And repeated episodes of intoxication or heavy drinking which impairs health—or the consistent use of alcohol as a coping mechanism in dealing with the problems of life to a degree of serious interference with an individual's effectiveness on the job, at home, in the community, or behind the wheel of a car—is alcohol abuse, and may raise the strong suggestion of alcoholism."

As early as 1957, the American Medical Association defined alcoholism as "a condition in which there is a deviation from a state of health." Said the AMA at that time:

> Alcoholism can be classified into (1) primary alcoholism, which includes (a) those patients who from the very first drink of an alcoholic beverage are unable to control their desire for it and (b) those who through use over a great many years have developed an inability to take a drink or leave it alone and have become like group (a) and (2) secondary alcoholism, which includes those who use alcohol for its sedative action as a means of escape from reality and, in particular, from their personal problems . . . . This secondary group comprises by far the majority of patients suffering from alcoholism; however, most alcoholic patients prefer to be in the primary group.

"Regardless of which group an individual belongs to," the AMA concluded, "when under the influence of alcohol, he is ill."

Two British authorities, Neil Kessel and Henry Walton, have attempted to break down the stages of alcohol addiction.[2] Their suggestive scheme might be helpful to families concerned about problem drinking:

Stage of Excessive Drinking
    More time spent in social drinking
    Drinks more nights of the week
    Sneaks drinks
    Takes stronger drinks than companions
    Adopts strategies to get more drinks
    Preoccupied with drinking
    Drinks to get relief from tension
    Increased tolerance
    Guilt over drinking
    Uses fabricated explanations to excuse social failures
    Needs drinks to perform adequately socially or at work
    Feels drink has become a necessity

Stage of Alcohol Addiction
    Onset of alcohol amnesia (blackouts)
    Loss of control—compulsive drinking
    Reduction in interests
    Drop in work efficiency
    Absenteeism
    Drunk in the daytime
    Reproof from employer or relatives
    Low self-esteem
    Remorse
    Compensatory bragging and generosity
    Financial extravagance
    Deceives family, debts made
    Increasing social isolation
    Aggressive outbursts
    Wife takes over responsibilities (Or vice versa)

Stage of Alcohol Addiction
    Deterioration in relations with wife
    Paranoid misinterpretations (unfounded suspicions)
    Self-pity
    Justifies drinking with self-deceptions
    Reduction of sexual drive
    Morbid jealousy

Drunk on weekends
Loss of job
Break-up of family
Morning tremulousness (the shakes)
Morning drinking
Conceals supplies of liquor
Repeated attempts to stop drinking
Suicidal impulses and attempts
Neglect of meals

Stage of Chronic Alcoholism
Physical and mental symptoms dominate
Loss of appetite, poor food intake
Continuous drinking
Tolerance diminishes
Prolonged confused thinking
Use of cheap wine and methylated spirits
Delirium Tremens
Goes to A.A. or seeks medical treatment
Serious physical diseases

"Not all alcoholics have the same symptoms," says A.A. "But many, at different stages in the illness, show these signs: They find that only alcohol can make them feel self-confident and at ease with other people; often want 'just one more' at the end of a party; look forward to drinking occasions and think about them a lot; get drunk when they had not planned to; try to control their drinking by changing types of liquor, going on the wagon or taking pledges; sneak drinks; lie about their drinking; hide bottles; drink at work (or in school); drink alone; have blackouts (that is, cannot remember the next day what they said or did the night before); drink in the morning to cure severe hangovers, guilty feelings and fears; fail to eat and become malnourished; get cirrhosis of the liver; shake violently, hallucinate or have convulsions when withdrawn from liquor."

One good rule of thumb to describe the alcoholic is that he (or she) is a person who drinks at the wrong time, in the wrong places, and for the wrong reasons. It isn't a matter of how much you drink or how long you have drunk. The crucial question which every alcoholic must ask is: What is drink doing to me?

However, the disease itself still lacks precise definition after years of extensive research. Consequently, the courts —no less than the medical profession—have been hampered in their work because there is "no agreement as to the meaning, manifestations, or treatment of 'alcoholism as a disease' " (Texas Supreme Court decision in Powell vs. Texas).

This lack eventually led the National Council on Alcoholism (1972) to establish criteria designed to diagnose the disease "on a standardized basis," but, at the same time, "avoid overdiagnosis." What it attempted to do was to "guard an individual from the presumption of alcoholism unless clear-cut reproducible data was available to confirm the diagnosis."

The criteria committee, headed by Dr. Samuel C. Kaim of the Veterans Administration's alcoholism staff in Washington, D.C., divided the manifestations of the disease into physiological and psychological symptoms and into major and minor criteria.

The NCA cited as examples of major criteria the presence of a withdrawal syndrome, tolerance to the effects of alcohol, the presence of alcoholic blackout periods, and continued drinking despite strong medical or social contraindication. Examples of minor criteria are such physiological disorders as cardiac arrhythmias and such behavioral patterns as gulping drinks, taking drinks surreptitiously, and automobile accidents.

"The satisfaction of one or more major criteria is sufficient for the diagnosis," the committee said. However, it warned that the physician must be careful to look for other causes when only "minor criteria" are evident.

No wonder that one member of the medical profession remarked that doctors were handed "another tough assignment" when it became generally accepted that alcoholism is a disease. "There also were new legal implications," he observed. "In the past, an abusive drunk was arrested and put in the coop. But in certain areas, he now must be hospitalized. After all, the sick deserve preferential treatment."

One interesting phenomenon with sticky legal implications involves the so-called alcoholic blackout. Does the heavy drinker really forget what he said and did the night before? Or does he merely wish to blot out what may be painful and unpleasant memories? Is a blackout a demonstrable fact? Or is it simply feigned?

A group of scientists at the Washington University Medical School in St. Louis sought to unravel this puzzle by giving ten persons, including eight alcoholics, sixteen to eighteen ounces of eighty-six proof bourbon over a four hour period. At intervals, each was shown one of eight toys and a scene from a motion picture.

Five of the alcoholics with a history of blackouts began to forget the toys and film thirty minutes after seeing them, beginning in the second and third hours of drinking. None of them had any recollection of either the toys or the film the next day.

This experiment led the researchers to conclude that, if a drinker forgets things he said or saw within a few minutes after consuming considerable liquor, he will not remember them the next day—and probably never will. But the experiment also raised the thorny question of what course the courts should take if a person accused of a crime insists that he was drunk and is unable to recall what happened during the commission of an offense.

Dr. Block has observed that about ten percent of alcoholics have a history of compulsion from their first drink, indicating a physical aberration in these individuals not yet understood. An equal number are psychotics for whom alcoholism is an overlay. The remaining eighty per cent, he said, comprise the bulk of American alcoholics—most of whom are unaware that they have the disease!

While it generally takes an average of ten years of heavy drinking to reach the point of alcohol addiction, some individuals become hooked after only three to five years of so-called moderate drinking. Others may imbibe heavily for twenty to thirty years before booze finally catches up with them. And then there is always the fellow who insists, "I was an alcoholic from my very first drink." A few people claim they were born drunks.

This raises the question of whether alcoholism can be inherited. Numerous studies have shown "the weed of compulsive drinking is more likely to flourish in a soil tainted with family alcoholism." At the Shadel Sanitarium in Seattle, for example, a survey of 500 alcoholics revealed that compulsive drinkers have a family history of alcoholism about four times that of the normal drinkers.

However, Dr. Fritz Kant, professor of neuropsychiatry at the University of Wisconsin, insists that the craving for alcohol cannot be transmitted in the egg or sperm. "A complex behavior pattern like that of alcoholism cannot be inherited," he says categorically. "We inherit genes but not characters. However, it cannot be denied that certain constitutional (inherited) traits may be partial determinants in a personality structure which leads to maladjustment and to the intemperate use of alcohol to escape from it."

Many Christians support the position that alcohol is the sole cause of alcoholism. Yet the Rev. Dr. James E. Royce, S. J., dean and professor of psychology at Seattle University, makes the observation that this notion is akin to saying that there would be no bank robberies without banks, and no divorces without marriage.

Most experts consider alcohol as an *agent* rather than the *cause* of alcoholism. "If it were the cause," says Gerald Knox, "everyone who drinks would become addicted to it. Which isn't, of course, the case."

Father Royce has suggested that alcoholism be accepted as a behavioral disorder, if not a disease, which in its later stages is marked by degeneration and a predictable course. He cites both the *pros* and *cons* of the now widely held disease concept from the standpoint of several observations:

Pros	Cons
It is a step forward from the sin concept to sickness.	Medically and technically alcoholism is not an allergy, but *like* an allergy.
The concept makes alcoholism a respectable object of scientific research.	There is no natural need for alcohol. The alcoholic can get over his physical compulsion.
The concept helps people see that the alcoholic cannot get over his problems alone, anymore than he could take out his own appendix.	No diagnosis is possible in the very early stages of alcoholism.
The concept is face-saving for both the alcoholic and his family.	The concept permits the alcoholic to rationalize that he cannot help himself—that he is "a hopeless case." Most illnesses are not self-inflicted.

Alcoholics Anonymous members often compare alcoholism to diabetes, pointing out that they are "allergic" to alcohol just as the diabetic is allergic to sugar. However, Father Royce notes, "the diabetic doesn't show the psychological habituation or the personality changes when he ingests sugar that are observed in the alcoholic when he takes a drink."

At the same time, he says, "Alcoholics Anonymous is correct in warning the alcoholic about the danger of the first drink. Once that drink reaches the cerebral cortex, judgment is impaired."

Royce also raises some questions regarding Jellinek's "five species" of alcoholism—a point shared by other authorities who consider these classifications too narrow to cover all of the manifestations of the disease.

In his historic study of *The Disease Concept of Alcoholism,* Jellinek had assigned Greek letters to distinguish between the various forms of the illness. Whatever their limitation, these classifications may help an alcoholic to identify the nature of his own problem within a framework suggested by a competent medical authority:

The *alpha* alcoholic has a purely psychological *continual* dependence upon the effect of alcohol to relieve bodily or emotional pain. He is undisciplined as to the time, place and amount of his drinking; but he does not suffer loss of control or the inability to abstain. Nor are there any signs of a progressive process.

The *beta* alcoholic may suffer from such physical maladies as gastritis, nervous disorders or cirrhosis of the liver without either physical or psychological dependence upon alcohol. Such a manifestation may be linked to a cultural group known for nutritional deficiencies, low family budgets, lowered productivity, and shortened life spans. However, withdrawal symptoms are unknown.

The *gamma* alcoholic shows clinical symptoms of (1) acquired increased tissue tolerance to alcohol, (2) adaptive cell metabolism, (3) withdrawal symptoms and physical dependence, and (4) loss of control. "In *gamma* alcoholism," says Jellinek, "there is a definite progression from psychological to physical dependence and marked behavior changes . . . . This species produces the greatest and most serious kinds of damage."

The *delta* alcoholic shows the first three characteristics of *gamma* alcoholism. However, instead of loss of control, there is the inability to abstain. While this may sound like a moot point, it means that the *delta* alcoholic cannot "go on the wagon" for even a day or two without the manifestation of withdrawal symptoms. This type of alcoholism may be evident in a culture like that of France where the daily use of wine is an accepted social custom.

The *epsilon* alcoholic is a periodic drinker. He may not drink for weeks or even months. But when he does go on a binge, he always ends up in serious trouble. This type of alcoholism is the least understood.

Jellinek points out that both *alpha* and *beta* alcoholism can develop into the *gamma* variety, the type most evident among members of Alcoholics Anonymous. He agrees that this species *appears* to predominate in the United States, Canada and other Anglo-Saxon countries. But he also notes that A.A. may have created its concept of alcoholism "in their own image." "I base this statement," he says, "on the fact that in a sample of slightly over 2,000 A.A. members I found thirteen percent who never experienced loss of control."

However, Father Royce still raises the question of whether Jellinek himself was unduly influenced in his study by the ready availability of A.A. members for his samplings. For example, he contends that the *delta* alcoholic cannot be isolated to countries such as France. "There are some Americans who never really get drunk," he says, "but always have that glow." He cites the case of a retired sailor who has his pension check mailed to a saloon.

Jellinek had also compiled a list of various theories put forth during a twenty year period that attempted to link alcoholism to a physiological factor. One investigator, for example, attributed the illness to innate susceptibility to alcohol, akin to a food allergy or drug idiosyncrasy. Others have suggested that alcoholism develops as a result of certain nutritional deficiencies. Still others have linked the disorder to lowered blood chloride levels, suggesting a perverted physiological craving for alcohol develops as a result of salt and water loss. But the trouble is, as Dr. Jellinek points out, none of these theories fully explains the mystery of alcohol addiction.

Father Royce is willing to concede that some alcoholics may be born with a physiological hereditary predisposition toward the disease. However, he says, "anyone who drinks long enough and hard enough will have a physical problem. It is not simply a nutritional matter. If it were, vitamins could be made available in every bar."

While he offers no simple solution to the problem, Royce points to differences in the pituitary gland of the alcoholic and the normal person. "Where normal people have distress signals from drinking too much," he says, "alcoholics seem to have gratification from greater tolerance." He further notes a distinction in the DNA pattern of some individuals, which gives rise to increased tolerance and different liver cells.

Therefore, Father Royce can only conclude: "There are now said to be thirty different types of alcoholics. (Not five as Jellinek suggested.) No two people are alike."

Whatever physiological factors may be involved, the alcoholic is in for serious trouble if he continues his drinking. There is always the possibility of cirrhosis of the liver. The fact that only a small percentage of excessive drinkers develop this condition led some medical authorities to conclude that it was probably caused by malnutrition rather than alcohol. However, Dr. Frank A. Seixas, the NCA's medical director, has now disclosed: "For the first time we're getting medical evidence which confirms the observations doctors have made—and dodged —for years; alcoholism and cirrhosis are very closely linked."

Dr. Jack D. Gordon, associate clinical professor at the University of California School of Medicine, has observed several physical reactions brought on by long and excessive use of alcohol:

    ... Tremors (the shakes), agitation, mild confusion (the onset coming in twelve to twenty-four hours after the last drink).

    ... Delirium tremens (the DTs), disorientation, various types of hallucinations (the onset coming within forty-eight to seventy-two hours after the last drink).

    ... Hyperactivity and tachycardia (rapid heart with as many as 130 beats per minute).

    ... Respiratory alkalosis caused by the ingestion of alcohol in large doses over a period of time. The heart and respiratory system compensate for the alcohol; then during withdrawal, these organs assert themselves and serious complications develop.

Gordon has also observed that alcoholics are often admitted to hospitals for other reasons—head injuries or trauma, acute gastrointestinal problems, acute infections, respiratory failure, or bacterial meningitis. Therefore, physicians must use caution in diagnosis.

There was a time when many people thought that a "wet brain" was the invention of Carrie Nation and her disciples. However, some solid medical evidence now exists to support the reality of this possibility. Moreover, a small group of alcoholics have been found to suffer from either Wernicke's syndrome or Korsakoff's syndrome. The first is indicated by incoordination and the inability to maintain balance in standing or walking, clouding of consciousness, and paralysis of eye muscles. The second is marked by polyneuritis, amnesia, and filling memory gaps with tales of imaginary events.

Some alcoholics may suffer from one or more of these conditions at one state, others at another. Some may escape such serious complications entirely. But in the background the possibility always looms that continued, uncontrolled drinking can reduce a man to either chronic

invalidism or death. Is a drink really worth your sanity—
or your life?

What can be done about the craving for alcohol?

Dr. Gordon tells of an experiment in which medical
students were paid to drink eight ounces of alcohol daily
for several days. They were also given proteins in their
diet. Yet tests showed that fatty liver tissue developed.
However, this condition quickly improved with abstinence.

On the other hand, other studies have demonstrated a
close relationship between nutritional deficiencies and the
use of alcohol. Dr. Roger J. Williams, University of Texas
biochemist, has noted that although alcoholics tend to
have a poor diet (often through neglect) the reverse is
also true: Bad diets create alcoholics. In his experiments
with rats, Dr. Williams discovered that a B vitamin deficiency manifested itself as an appetite-mechanism disorder and the rats ended up craving alcohol instead of
good food. A similar effect was noted at Loma Linda University in California, where a "typical U.S. diet"—high
in carbohydrates—turned rats into alcoholics. In some
cases, massive doses of the B vitamins and niacin amide
have reportedly resulted in spectacular reduction of the
physical craving for alcohol.

There is an old story around A.A. about the fellow
who asked his sponsor what to do when he got thirsty.
"Have a milkshake," he replied. "If you still have the
craving, have another one. If you still want to drink,
you're not an alcoholic. You're nuts!"

Some alcoholics will tell you there is more than a grain
of truth in this tale.

But A.A. members have also learned there just isn't any
magic pill to stop a man from drinking. In Sigmund
Freud's day, there were claims that cocaine might be a
cure for alcoholism. In our own, some thought LSD might
reduce the craving. But the most common fallacy today
is to substitute tranquilizers for booze. Unhappily, count-

less alcoholics have ended up with cross-addictions or have gotten hooked on a drug just as destructive as alcohol itself.

Great claims have also been made for drugs known as metronidazole and propranolol hydrochloride. But even their staunchest supporters admit these drugs may only be helpful for those who want to stop drinking. The rest just stop taking the drug and return to the bottle.

This holds true for Antabuse and Temposil, the two deterrent drugs often prescribed for the treatment of alcoholism. "When a patient takes one of the deterrent drugs," says Marvin Block, "he cannot drink alcohol without becoming violently sick. Thus when he takes a pill, the question of drinking for the day is settled. Temptation is removed."

However, Dr. Block advises patients taking these drugs to simultaneously undergo psychotherapy. For there are always the possibilities that the alcoholic will either skip the pill and return to the bottle, or that he will attempt to ingest alcohol before the drug has completely left his system. This can cause disastrous results.

A New York City policeman, himself a member of A.A., tells the story of being called into the Times Square area to investigate what appeared to be a "death by natural causes." At the scene, he found an Army officer who had died there on the street. Rummaging through the man's effects, the patrolman found military orders for the victim to proceed from Grand Central Station to the Port Authority Bus Terminal enroute to his next assignment. He also discovered the man was taking Antabuse.

The investigation led the patrolman into one of the nearby bars. The bartender immediately recognized the victim's description. He told the officer he thought it was a little strange that the customer ordered six double shots of whiskey at one time. "All I could figure out," said the policeman later, "is the guy thought one or two drinks would hurt him on top of the Antabuse—but six would get him over the hump. He was wrong. They killed him."

Is alcoholism caused by a demon? Or is it the manifestation of a complex disease?

The following story, now yellow with age, may give those on both sides of the controversy something to ponder.

Many years ago a well-known clergyman stood up at a church meeting and spoke favorably of wine. He contended that its use was genteel, healthful, and within the limits of Scripture. When he sat down, an old man asked permission to speak.

"A young friend of mine," he said, "who had long been intemperate, was at length prevailed upon, to the great joy of his friends, to take the pledge of entire abstinence from all that could intoxicate. He kept the pledge faithfully for some time, struggling with his habit fearfully, till one evening in a social party glasses of wine were handed around. They came to a clergyman present, who took a glass, saying a few words in vindication of the practice.

" 'Well,' thought the young man, 'if a clergyman can take wine and justify it so well, why not I?' So he took a glass. It instantly rekindled his slumbering appetite. And after a downward course, he died of delirium tremens—a raving madman."

Then the old man paused for a minute before he was able to add: "That young man was my son. And that clergyman was the Reverend Doctor who has just addressed this assembly."

The story, apocryphal though it might be, points up several things. So-called "tolerance" to social drinking may do as much harm to the alcoholic as any plea for total abstinence. But this boy might have been spared had an organization like A.A. existed in his day.

Yet the most important point is this: For reasons not

yet fully understood, alcoholics have lost control. One drink is too many; and a thousand isn't enough. Or, as Selden Bacon put it more positively, "Alcoholics do not drink."

6

The Id Meets the Odd

> *"For the flesh lusteth against the Spirit, and the Spirit against the flesh: and these are contrary the one to the other: so that ye cannot do the things that ye would . . . But the fruit of the Spirit is love, joy, peace, longsuffering, gentleness, goodness, faith, meekness, temperance: against such there is no law"* (Galatians 5: 17, 22, 23).
>
> *"For God hath not given us the spirit of fear; but of power, and of love, and of a sound mind"* (II Timothy 1: 7).

FATHER SEAN will allow that while he can no longer drink whiskey he can still drink wine.

Only the Emerald Isle itself holds fonder memories for the good priest than those quiet evenings when he would unburden himself of sacerdotal responsibility over a fifth of good Scotch.

The fabled glories of this Highland brew were the one concession he would make to the British. For he much preferred the delicate bouquet of Johnnie Walker to the soapy taste of Irish whiskey.

So great was Father's affection for the amber liquid that even the monsignor heard about it. "Sean, me boy," said the prelate one day, "something's got to be done about your drinking. It just doesn't look good for you to lead a confraternity class half in the bag."

The monsignor, it seems, had heard about a place where those who love the sauce will come to hate it. To be sure, Sean questioned such a remote possibility. But dutifully he packed his bags and headed for an all-expense-paid vacation to the sanatorium.

The morning of his departure, Sean poured himself a good stiff drink. He was shaking badly; but somehow his lilting brogue managed to assume an almost stentorian quality as he lifted the tumbler to the sunlight and ceremoniously declared: "Refrain tonight, and that shall lend a kind of easiness to the next abstinence: the next more easy; for use almost can change the stamp of nature."

For some reason, his mind was still on the tragic figure of Hamlet as he curled up in the back seat of the car for the long drive to the hospital. "Good night, sweet prince," he yawned. "And flights of angels sing thee to thy rest."

Sean had reconciled himself to the idea that booze would be off-limits at the "drying out farm." He had of course heard that someone would be glad to slip you a bottle for a price. But he had made his decision: He would try to play the game by the rules—even if it killed him. "Refrain tonight," he mused. "And that shall lend a kind of easiness to the next abstinence."

But there was no need for martyrs at the sanatorium. In fact, he had barely entered its well-scrubbed grounds when a doctor said knowingly: "Father, you look as if you could use a drink."

Sweeter words could only be heard in Erin's happy halls!

Sean awoke the next morning and soon was informed about the type of treatment employed by the medical staff. He would be allowed to drink at prescribed intervals. There was only one stipulation: He would be given a small injection of a nauseant drug before each drinking episode. "We call it aversion therapy," explained the doctor. "We are aiming for behavior modification by so sensitizing the nervous system that alcohol will become obnoxious to you."

Sean had heard all about Pavlog's dog. But school book knowledge ill-prepared him for what lay in store. He gladly submitted to the first needle so that he could get down to some serious drinking. In a few minutes, however, he found himself retching violently. He suddenly lost any more taste for booze.

Treatment continued on a daily basis. He was told that he must cultivate acceptance of his disability on medical grounds—that he would always be one drink away from catastrophe. The aversion therapy itself was meant to arouse within him a distaste for the sight, smell and taste of alcohol in any form. After twenty-three needles he went back to his parish sober if not serene.

Then an amazing thing occurred in the life of Father Sean. It is true that he could no longer stand the sight of the hard stuff. Even the thought of whiskey made him sick to his stomach. "But I wonder about wine," he pondered, as he stood in the sacristy one day after Mass.

Sean had been physically sober for several months; but the psychological craving had remained. Slowly he lifted the wine to his lips, and, feeling no ill effects, he never put the bottle down again until he entered Alcoholics Anonymous.

A somewhat more "shocking" form of aversion therapy is currently being employed at the Patton State Hospital in San Bernardino, California, where alcoholic patients are asked to choose between total abstinence and a return to so-called social drinking.

Then they begin their five-week treatment program by being ushered into a well-stocked cocktail lounge. There are soft lights, a polished mahogany bar, unobtrusive music—and drinks served by a comely barmaid at the taxpayers' expense.

That first visit to the lounge can be a shocking experience for these long-time drinkers who always thought they grew more witty and charming under the influence of alcohol. They are allowed to order as many as sixteen one-ounce drinks—before a videotape replay of their behavior is flashed on the screen to demolish all illusions about their wit and charm.

In succeeding sessions, those who have opted for a return to social drinking are permitted to consume as many as three mixed drinks without receiving a painful shock from electrodes attached to the hands. But the drinks must be sipped—not gulped—and each drink must last at least twenty minutes. Violations of these simple ground rules brings a jab of harmless pain.

Treatment is even more dramatic—and shocking—for those who want to abstain from alcohol entirely.

They receive a sharp electrical jolt every time they order a drink. They are subjected to a continuous shock for even holding a glass harmlessly in their hands!

Psychologists Halmuth Schaefer and Mark Sobell, who head the Patton State program, reject the notion that alcoholism is based on a physiological craving. They rather insist that problem drinking is a psychological ailment that can be arrested by behavior modification techniques.

Alcoholism, they say, represents a learned response to stress. Some people may react to anxiety by punching somebody in the nose, walking around the block, or overeating. The alcoholic picks up a drink.

But, say Schaefer and Sobell, what has been learned can be unlearned. And they attempt to achieve this goal by the harmless—although painful—series of electrical shocks.

Another aversion technique is being trumpeted by psychologist S. H. Lovibond of the University of New South Wales. Actually, this method is as old as Noah and follows in the tradition of Aristophanes' comedy, "Lysistrata."

Gals Down Under are simply advised by Dr. Lovibond to make their errant husbands choose between booze and the marriage bed.

"We don't tell the wives," says the professor, "that withholding sex is one aversion technique, but each is left to devise her own method. Quite a few have devised sex withholding to help an alcoholically addicted husband conquer his weakness."

Dr. Lovibond, who also uses electro-shock therapy in some cases, claims a sixty percent success rate. But nothing is said of the failures.

There are many alcoholics who couldn't care less about sex after the libido has been anesthetized by ninety proof. The one great love of their lives is the bottle. Others might well use such a technique as an excuse for continued drinking. Some might even go so far as to search for more compatible companions of the opposite sex. It's a risky business, to say the least.

But the denial of conjugal rights may tell more about the spouse of the alcoholic than about the alcoholic himself. Some wives may be looking for just such an option so that they do not have to deal with sexual hang-ups in their own lives. Others might use this technique as one more weapon in their arsenal to dominate or emasculate their husbands. In any case, some wives may be in need of professional help themselves.

It is for reasons such as these that analytically-oriented psychotherapists consider most behavioral approaches to alcoholism therapy of only limited value. Aversion techniques may aid in the recovery process, they say, but they fail to deal with underlying and often unconscious causes.

Most behaviorists themselves readily concede that their techniques work only with the properly motivated patient. But the issue goes much deeper than that.

Sigmund Freud, for example, was the first to interpret all neuroses and emotional conflicts in terms of the so-called Oedipus complex or some other form of arrested sexual development. Freud suggested that alcoholism represents a regression to the oral stage of psychosexuality in which the infant is dependent and free of responsibility. His aberrant behavior is indicative of an unconscious desire for the breast or the feeding bottle. This longing for oral gratification is said to be repressed; but it causes intense anxiety which drives the problem drinker to alcohol in an effort to escape his great psychic pain.

Howard Clinebell finds no difficulty in accepting Freud's interpretation because of what he calls "the essential orality of alcoholism." But he goes on to make a suggestion which has bearing for the teaching and witnessing Church:

> Would it not embark on a comprehensive program of parent education as a central focus of its work, making the discoveries of the psychologists concerning the emotional hungers of children, from the very dawn of life on, easily available to all its parents? Through such a program parents could come to see that healthy personality is "homemade" and that an ounce of mother is worth a pound of psychiatrist.
>
> Such parent education should put particular emphasis on helping the parents of infants to satisfy their babies' oral needs, the babies being allowed abundant sucking and given cuddling as well as generous amounts of TLC, tender loving care. By helping parents to do that which they basically want to do but often cannot—namely, raise children who are mentally, emotionally, and spiritually healthy—the Church would help to prevent alcoholism at its very roots.[3]

Another Freudian insight which has some bearing on alcohol addiction is known as the pain-pleasure principle. In the case of the alcoholic, problem drinkers experience pleasure during some phases of their drinking careers, and that search for pleasure is deeply involved in their addiction. But this does not negate the fact that terrible psychological pain is also present.

The problem is that both the theologian and the therapist often have more difficulty *in themselves* dealing with the pleasure as opposed to the pain. Clinebell cites the sage observation of Giorgio Lolli, onetime medical director of the Yale Plan Clinic, to support this contention. "An even dim awareness of the pleasurable connotations of some phases of the drinking episode," said Lolli, "cannot fail to stir up anxieties in those therapists whose conscious and, even more, whose unconscious life is governed by the principle: 'I shall help the sufferer and punish the celebrant.' " Ditto for many well-meaning clergymen and Christian laymen!

Phyllis Perera, a member of the pastoral counseling staff of the Postgraduate Center for Mental Health, New York City, tells her clergymen-students that they must always remember that with Freud they are dealing with exegesis; the psychoanalytic theories after him, she adds, represent commentary.

This observation is especially pertinent when those interested in alcohol addiction—including the problem drinker and his family—undertake a study of psychoanalytic theories about the illness since the day of Sigmund Freud. For an uncritical acceptance of any theory can only lead the alcoholic into deeper despair and lull the therapist into seeking a simple solution to an extremely complex problem.

Karl Menninger has linked alcoholism to an unconscious urge to destroy oneself. For disciples of Alfred Adler, alcoholism arises from the individual's desire to eliminate powerful feelings of inferiority while escaping responsibility and social involvement. Sandor Rado noted that the euphoria produced by alcohol is a unique source of satisfaction in a life otherwise ridden with boredom, frustration and disappointment. By drinking with abandonment, Rado suggests, the alcoholic can fulfill his fantasies of omnipotence and become, at least temporarily, the unchallanged master of his own disorganized world.

More recent investigations have centered on the broader issue of what scientists call *homeostasis*. This simply means that all organisms—including man—seek to maintain an internal balance or equilibrium. An example of this principle is evident in the body's tendency to maintain an even temperature, despite temperature changes in the surrounding environment. This same principle can also be seen in man's psychological nature. All of us have certain needs or drives which must be gratified. But the question is whether these needs are to be met through healthy interaction or by neurotic and destructive behavioral patterns, which are *learned* and become *reinforced* by constant practice.

Such studies invariably drive the investigator back to the original thinking of Sigmund Freud. Otto Fenichel, for example, merely builds on the foundation of his master when he suggests that alcoholics are characterized by their "oral and narcissistic pre-morbid personalities." By this he seems to believe that drinking somehow tends to satisfy the passive and dependence drives of the alcoholic.

Other experts simply conclude that drinking reduces anxiety, stress, and worry. They tend to suggest that the alcoholic is distinguished from the social drinker only by degree. "It is usually assumed," says John J. Conger of the University of Colorado School of Medicine, ". . . that in these cases the motivation for drinking is more intense and insistent, and may even be qualitatively different, than in the case of the casual social drinker."

Scientific interest in the problem of alcohol addiction has produced a series of enlightening studies. For example, Masserman and Yum discovered that a group of trained cats developed fear reactions whenever they approached their food and were met by air blasts or electrical shocks. But these same animals fed on signal after they had been given a good stiff dose of alcohol. No wonder so many sober Milquetoasts say that a few drinks make them "feel ten feet tall."

Anthropologist David Horton's cross-cultural study of drinking behavior in nonliterate societies carries its own message for harried Horatio Algers involved in the daily rat race. "The strength of the drinking response in any society," Horton found, "tends to vary directly with the level of anxiety in the society."

But that still doesn't explain the phenomenon of a man whose "lost weekends" bring him far more pain than pleasure. As Dr. Conger observes: "The man who is effectively alienating his employer, his wife, and his friends hardly seems to be socially rewarded for his drinking." The Colorado psychologist suggests that such socially punitive behavior might be explained either in terms of the amount of drive and conflict, or in terms of the immediacy of reward. "The promise of an ice cream cone after supper," he says, "is frequently more effective in encouraging a child to behave than the distant image of a new bicycle for Christmas."

What role heredity plays in the shaping of an alcoholic is still an unsettled question. But a recent article in *The American Journal of Psychiatry* (March, 1972) suggests that a tendency toward alcoholism may not be dissimilar to a propensity toward diabetes. In that article, doctors Marc A. Shuckit, Donald A. Goodwin, and George Winokur reported that their study of sixty-nine alcoholic patients in two St. Louis hospitals indicated that genes may have more bearing than geography in the evolution of the problem drinker.

Some of the patients in this study were born and reared by alcoholic parents. Others were born to drinkers but reared by teetotaling relatives or adoptive parents. Nonetheless, the investigators discovered, children born to at least one alcoholic parent did not receive much protection against the disease by being reared in a booze-free home. The incidence of alcoholism among people of this background was six times greater than it was among those whose natural parents were not problem drinkers.

Certainly the most controversial—and potentially dangerous—psychoanalytic theory concerning alcoholism attributes the illness to latent homosexuality. One of the first to introduce this notion was Sandor Ferenczi, Freud's disciple from Budapest. The idea was later embellished to include the Oedipus complex and fear of castration, both basic to Freudian psychology.

Psychotherapists who accept the notion of latent homosexuality in alcoholics often point to the fact that men appear to find partial satisfaction for their alleged and unacknowledged homosexual drives in the male-dominated environment of the neighborhood gin mill. But it can also be argued rather persuasively that many problem drinkers, at least early in their drinking careers, engage in a never-ending round of bar hopping in a frantic search for a girl with whom they can have casual heterosexual involvement. It would seem that the ghost of Sandor Ferenczi would feel more at home in the men's bar of the Twenties than in the dimly lit cocktail lounges of the Swinging Seventies!

However, this does not negate the generally accepted theoretical position that alcoholics may have unresolved sexual conflicts they are not consciously aware of. For example, Kessel and Walton cite instances of heterosexual men finding themselves in bed with another male after a hard night's drinking bout. They further contend that vocal abhorrence of "queers" may actually mask the repression of unresolved homosexual tendencies. If permitted a Freudian slip, they might say: "The lady doth protest too much, methinks."

But this entire question has probably sparked more emotional conflict than it has been able to resolve. "In my opinion," says Lincoln Williams, "this is a glaring instance of the danger of trying to make the facts fit a theory instead of deriving a theory from the facts. No doubt sexual conflicts and repression sometime play a part in producing alcoholic addiction as sometime they contribute to other forms of neurotic behavior; but my experience leaves me in no doubt that the proportion of overt or latent homosexuality among alcoholics is no greater than that to be found in any other cross-section of the community." Moreover, he adds, "no other form of sexual repression or inhibition is alone sufficient to account for the addiction."

What is unfortunate about this tragically-misunderstood theoretical concept is that it gives the alcoholic with doubts about his sexual identity just one more good excuse to drink. He needs to know, as Lionel Ovesey points out, that there are nonsexual elaborations of male homosexuality—dependency, power, aggression, competition, domination, submission, and status. These personality components must be distinguished from the purely sexual motivation of orgastic satisfaction. In a word, no one is likely to call an old-fashioned drunk a "queer"—unless, of course, he hits someone over the head with his pocketbook in a barroom brawl!

In their experience, however, Kessel and Walton have isolated three types of sexual problems found among many alcoholics: (1) those with little sexual drive who may turn to drink to increase sexual ardor or to escape the recriminations of the self or the spouse, (2) those who use alcohol to reduce anxiety related to contact with the opposite sex or with the sexual act itself—fear that intercourse is physically debilitating or a carrier of disease, and (3) others who make the bottle the companion of such deviations as homosexuality, sadism, fetishism, or voyeurism. In all of these instances, professional help would be a distinct aid to recovery.

It would be highly erroneous to assume that male alcoholics alone are burdened by sexual hang-ups which contribute to aberrant drinking behavior. The fact is, as Edith S. Lisansky points out, "there is a not too clearly stated assumption that alcoholism in women and sexual promiscuity are somehow related." Against this largely unsupported generalization, the Yale psychologist points to several studies (Levine, Curran, et. al.) which indicate that sexual frigidity may be a factor in problem drinking among women. Again, professional help may be called for in such cases.

However, Dr. Lisansky believes, "alcoholism among women is more likely to be associated with some concrete situation than is true among men. The inference is that precipitating circumstances play more of a role in the development of alcoholism among women. Asked in a recent study about the circumstances surrounding the beginning of problem drinking, twice as many alcoholic women as men cited a specific past experience: a parent's death, a divorce, an unhappy love affair, a postpartum depression, and so forth. Social environmental pressures may indeed play more of a precipitating role in women's alcoholism."

This distinguished authority on female problem drinking also points out that Freud's famous dictum that "anatomy is destiny" may have some bearing on alcoholism among women. Dr. Lisansky cites studies which indicate a relationship between problem drinking and feminine physiological functions—menstruation, childbirth, and menopause. But, she says, "what would seem to be of far greater consequence in the development of alcoholism is the woman patient's emotional adjustment to and acceptance of these feminine physiological functions."

The fact is that an overwhelming number of alcoholics

—male and female alike—can always manage to rationalize their need for the next drink. This was forcefully brought home by the A.A. gal who once remarked: "I always blamed my drinking on the fact that I had no children until I met the woman who said she would have never used alcohol if it hadn't been for those darn kids."

This tendency to rationalize has been at the heart of the uneasy relationship between alcoholic and orthodox analyst. The alcoholic isn't concerned in the least about unconscious Oedipal strivings; he is only interested in when and where he will get his next drink. Yet he has lied so much about his drinking that the analyst often finds it next to impossible to obtain an accurate case history. As a result, many alcoholics abandon psychotherapy after one or two visits, preferring instead to invest their time and money with an expert on all questions human, political, social and economic: the local bartender, whose ministrations will last as long as a guy has the price of a drink!

Harry M. Tiebout, the first psychiatrist to recognize the work of Alcoholics Anonymous, was also the first psychiatrist to recognize that orthodox psychoanalytic methods were virtually useless in the treatment of a shaking, sweating, retching mass of humanity.

Unfortunately, Dr. Tiebout suggests, the psychotherapist is often as much a slave to his training as the alcoholic is to the bottle. "The individual either changes and begins to function, or he remains rigid and becomes discouraged, disillusioned, and skeptical about the prospects of working with the alcoholic," he says. "The unfortunate truth is that, as far as psychiatrists are concerned, a sizable majority never quite make the grade. They always seem like fish out of water."

Dr. Tiebout contends that the basic problem with so many psychiatrists is that they expect methods which are successful in other cases to work equally as well with alcoholics. "The present-day psychiatrist is steeped in the methods of modern medicine," he observes. "Whenever you encounter illness, you search for the cause, then you treat the cause and cure the illness. That is just as true for psychiatric ailments as it is for physical conditions. Treatment is directed toward etiology.

"When a person so oriented hits alcoholism," he says, "he is out of luck—only he does not know it. . . . He bypasses the disease and looks for causes. He ends up talking about earlier experiences and never gets close to this patient or the illness. His training is a hindrance, instead of a help. He must revamp his sights, or he is lost."

Dr. Tiebout's own enlightenment came after he discovered that alcoholic patients routinely complained that their talks with psychiatrists were almost uniformly unhelpful. "The complaint was," he says, "that the psychiatrists never talked about the drinking and seemed to minimize its importance, which was duck soup for the alcoholic, but, in the long run, not very effective. The routine history-taking approach seemed to have many strikes against it.

"Then," he says, "A.A. came along with a program to stop drinking; causation was ignored; the focus was all on treatment. Medicine's insistence on treating causes was disregarded, not wittingly to be sure, but the emphasis was on stopping the drinking and helping the individual to achieve and maintain that end. Like the treatment by surgery, the causes were irrelevant in meeting the immediate issues. Instead of the scalpel, there was the A.A. program. Instead of the infected appendix being removed, the individual was told to stop drinking, or stated in another way, liquor was removed from his life."

The startling success of Alcoholics Anonymous led Dr. Tiebout to the conclusion that any treatment of the problem drinker must be remedial. "There is no present value in getting at the causes and correcting them," he says, "because the net result of such an endeavor would be to enable the person to drink normally. While such a goal may be achieved in some far-off millennium, its attainment in the immediate future is absolutely unlikely. Any therapy devoted to such a goal is admittedly unrealistic. *Everyone acknowledges that there is no present cure, that the only remedy is total sobriety. The person does not learn how to handle liquor—he stops using it.*"

But the big problem for both the alcoholic and the analyst is that the problem drinker is a past master in employing various dodges and stratagems to excuse his aberrant behavior. "Defense reactions are found in every psychological illness," Dr. Tiebout notes. "The alcoholic has the same defenses as others, plus a sturdy crop of his own, arising from the special nature of his ailment. Until the practitioner develops some dexterity in penetrating the wall surrounding the alcoholic, he can anticipate little progress."

What Tiebout seems to suggest is that psychotherapy might be far more productive after the alcoholic has been dried out and achieved some degree of sobriety in A.A.

Ruth Fox, another long-time friend of A.A., echoes the sentiments of her distinguished colleague. "I gave up psychoanalysis as a technique for treating alcoholism," she says. "I still think it can be useful for some alcoholics *after* they have established some stable A.A. sobriety.

"But from my own experience," she adds, "I have seen that simply understanding (the alcoholic's) problems certainly cannot turn any alcoholic into a social drinker!"

Dr. Fox tells the story of an alcoholic psychiatrist and psychoanalyst who once was her patient. The man had seventeen years of psychoanalysis, but his drinking just kept getting worse. One day he explained his basic problem to his therapist: "One martini, and all your insight goes right out the window!"

Dr. Fox has earned the reputation of a no-nonsense

psychotherapist who refuses to coddle her patients, knowing that they have built up an elaborate set of defenses to excuse their drinking. At the same time, she has endeavored to keep an open mind on treatment methods—having used and discarded LSD, hypnotherapy, psychoanalytically-oriented group therapy, megavitamin therapy, and encounter groups. Today she employs counseling, psychodrama, informational therapy and Antabuse. But she still "pushes" A.A. as the cornerstone of her treatment.

Any psychoanalytical approach to the problem of uncontrolled drinking must come to grips with at least three realities:

One, A.A. has always claimed that alcoholism is a threefold disease—physical, emotional, spiritual. Psychotherapists, on the other hand, have generally minimized the spiritual and/or moral component, preferring instead to focus on such matters as Oedipus, narcissism, and the id-ego conflict originating as early as the oral period.

Unfortunately, self-awareness of conflict between the id (man's instinctual drives) and his superego (conscience) generally have little effect on the drinking pattern of an alcoholic who is guilt-ridden because of illicit sex or some other skeleton in his emotional closet. Alcoholics Anonymous contends that he will never find sobriety—much less serenity—until he confesses "the exact nature of his wrongs" and gets "the monkey off of his back." For it recognizes that the superego—or conscience —is the one part of the human personality which "becomes soluble in alcohol."

Two, the temptation among psychotherapists is to fall prey to what has been described as "reductionism" in the diagnosis and treatment of alcoholism.

Dr. Milton Kapit of the Postgraduate Center for Mental Health tells the engaging story of a Viennese photographer who was brought to trial on murder charges involving his father. Father and son had taken a walk, and the old man suddenly and mysteriously fell to his death as both ascended a mountain. People in the town below knew that there had been "bad blood" between the two men. Consequently, the son was charged with his father's murder.

The case might well have been long-forgotten were it not for the fact that the prosecution appealed to no less an authority than Sigmund Freud to bolster the rather shaky circumstantial evidence. In building his case, the prosecutor noted that Dr. Freud had suggested in his use of the myth of Oedipus that every male child harbors an unconscious wish to kill the father. In this instance, the prosecutor claimed, the son had actually acted out this unconscious desire. But, says Dr. Kapit, "Freud never suggested that the Oedipus will be acted out in this way, anymore than a boy will act out his unconscious desire to go to bed with his mother."

This is an example of the "reductionism" that psychotherapists deplore in amateur psychologists. Yet they themselves are often guilty of the same shortcoming in reducing the various forms of alcohol addiction to a neat set of psychoanalytical categories.

Three, there just ain't any stereotype of the alcoholic. It is as unreasonable to speak of a uniform "alcoholic personality" as it is to talk about the "lazy Mexican," the "radical Black," or the "shyster Jew." Alcoholics are as different as any other segment of the total population.

Lincoln Williams says categorically that experience has shown most convincingly that problem drinkers must be treated as individuals—not as a group. "In the treatment of alcoholism the importance of taking into account the personal characteristics of each patient cannot be overemphasized," he insists. "This being so, why do we so often hear the remark, 'He is a typical drunk'?"

Yet it cannot be denied that there are certain personality traits which are common to many alcoholics. For example, Frederick S. (Fritz) Perls and other members of the Gestalt school of therapy appear to share Freud's belief that problem drinking has its roots in a regression to the oral stage of personality development. This is how the imitable Fritz and colleagues Ralph Hefferline and Paul Goodman describe the alcoholic:

He is a bottle baby, a gulper, reluctant to take solid food and chew it. This applies to the steak on his platter and to the larger problems of his life situation. He wants his solutions in liquid form, pre-prepared, so that he need but drink them down.

Socially, he wants to enter into immediate confluence without preparatory contact with the other person. His acquaintance of the moment becomes a pal to whom he will "pour out his heart." He by-passes those parts of his personality which would exercise discrimination; and then, on the basis of these superficial social contacts, he comes forth with impatient, extravagant demands.

Just as uncritically, he takes in social reproaches and accepts them as coming from himself, for he has a strong self-aggressive conscience. He may silence it by drowning it in alcohol, but when he awakes, its vindictiveness is redoubled. Since his aggression is not used in attacking his physical food or his problems, the surplus which is not invested in his conscience often turns outward in surly, irrelevant fights.[4]

It is interesting that Fritz Perls contends that alcoholism, although complicated by many ramifications, "is muscularly anchored in oral underdevelopment." By this he means that the problem drinker must literally learn to chew solid food. While he would undoubtedly deny the inference, Fritz sounds strangely similar to the writer of Hebrews by insisting that the mature person—no less than the sturdy saint—is distinguished by his ability to give up milk for solid food (Hebrews 5: 12).

Mike, a broadcast engineer, provides a good example of what Perls has described in theoretical terms. He has maintained his sobriety for several years by remaining active in Alcoholics Anonymous. Unfortunately, Mike is a member of that small minority that sometimes uses A.A. in the same way that he formerly used the bottle. He must certainly take his own inventory; but it would appear that he is on a prolonged "dry drunk." For he has never grown up.

Mike, the bottle baby and gulper, blames all of his problems on Jane, who gave up a nursing career to care for a family. So disoriented has family life become that Mike seldom comes home for dinner. To do so makes him physically ill. "I get about two miles from the house," he says, "and I have to pull the car over to the side of the road. I feel as though my stomach is tied in knots, and I just want to puke. I can't stand the thought of going home."

What Mike seems to be doing is to project his own self-hatred and low self-esteem to his wife and children. He believes that Jane is the only one who needs help, although he thinks his oldest daughter is somewhat of a "weirdo" because of her dress and occasional use of marijuana. But underneath Mike is a tragically frightened man. He is filled with both fear and resentment because, as he puts it, he will be "an old man before the last kid leaves the nest." Meanwhile, Mike himself remains an emotional infant.

Authoritarian to the point of arrogance at home, Mike is the image of charm among A.A. friends. He can talk endlessly about such masculine pursuits as skydiving and deer hunting; and, although he is up to his ears in debt, no one is more loquacious when it comes to the condition of the stock market. But Mike's reticence becomes apparent when the conversation shifts to his own deep inner feelings. Meanwhile, A.A. friends cannot understand just how Mike has been able to put up with Jane for all of these years.

This story provides an example of neurotic interaction between a couple which demands professional help. Alcoholics Anonymous might help Mike to deal with some of his interpersonal troubles; but it makes no claim of expertise in dealing with unconscious intrapsychic conflict. It gave Mike a marginal type of sobriety; but the right therapist might be able to give this couple some degree of real serenity.

At the other extreme is the case of an A.A. gal who has described her first thirty-four years of life as "a series of well learned negative feelings and attitudes." "So ingrained were these into my total personality," she says, "that seven and a half years of intensive psychotherapy, plus six months in a psychiatric institute, did no more than give me self-sanction to attempt a nearly successful suicide and to sink further into severe states of depression and anxiety."

This woman left therapy to continue drinking behind the locked doors of her home. She also became addicted to tranquilizers and sedatives as she watched three marriages dissolve in the alcoholic fog. Release came only upon her introduction to the A.A. way of life. She not only found sobriety, she says, but "when an old negative thought does come, I tell it, 'You can visit, but you can't stay.' "

Here is an example of a woman who claims to have achieved some degree of emotional maturity, ego identity and conflict resolution through the supportive fellowship of Alcoholics Anonymous—*after* she had made what she *perceived* to be a serious attempt to reach these goals with the help of psychotherapy. However, the question can still be raised as to whether the degree of self-awareness gained in therapy contributed far more than she may realize to her ready acceptance of the A.A. way of life.

This story also points up that therapists and problem drinkers alike often err in putting the cart before the horse. While the therapist may dismiss the drinking to get at its cause, the alcoholic is likely to accept any form of treatment that does not interfere with his obsessive infatuation with the bottle.

Bob's experience is a case in point. His aberrant behavior led a team of v.a. psychiatrists to diagnose him as a paranoiac schizophrenic, too often a catch-all phrase used to describe alcoholics whose symptoms demand too much time and energy for already burdened psychotherapists. Consequently, they declared him 100 percent disabled and handed him a massive supply of Librium to control his emotional outbursts. His family apologetically explained to neighbors that Bob was "sick," while Bob himself came to see himself as "hopeless" as he continued to drown his sorrows in booze.

It was only after Bob was admitted to a hospital specializing in the treatment of alcoholics that a psychiatrically oriented physician was able to convince him that his primary problem was uncontrolled drinking. Upon discharge from the hospital, Bob joined A.A. He has had a couple "slips" and sometimes becomes depressed. "But," says his still unbelieving wife, "Bob is a new man."

Ken had a somewhat different experience. He just *knew* that he was "nuts" when his long-suffering spouse prevailed upon him to see a psychiatrist about his drinking. Ken thinks he got gypped for his money; but actually he got the best bargain of his life in one visit to a "shrink." The doctor didn't even bother to take a case history. He just told Ken about A.A. and suggested that he look into the program. "I had one slip after going to that psychiatrist," he says. "But that visit spoiled my drinking. It made me face my real problem. I think that is the reason why I never had any problem with the A.A. program from the moment I joined the fellowship." That was six years ago.

While the experts agree that there is no such thing as an "alcoholic personality," they have observed certain

141

personality traits which are common to many problem drinkers. For example, David Shapiro, author of *Neurotic Styles* and former chief psychologist at the Austen Riggs Center in Stockbridge, Massachusetts, has described many alcoholic patients as either "passive" or "impulsive." In both cases, they either "give in" to temptation or "give in" to pressure.

Dr. Shapiro contends that alcoholics often follow what he calls the "marionette" pattern of behavior, looking upon themselves as the hapless victims of historical—or childhood—circumstances which serve as a ready excuse for uncontrolled drinking. While he concedes that there might be some theoretical justification for this rationalization, he also argues that knowledgeable therapists "cannot quite swallow the idea of their innocence and cannot help noticing that they do not altogether regret what their impulses choose to do with them."

Lionel M. Lazowick, chief of the Eden Alcoholism Clinic in Alameda County, California, is among the experts who warn against the temptation of building a mythological profile of the typical alcoholic. However, he has isolated certain characteristics often found in problem drinkers, as well as in other members of the general population.

Dr. Lazowick claims that alcoholics often demonstrate a *low frustration tolerance* when their wishes, needs or demands are not immediately gratified. "This tendency shows itself by withdrawal, anger, tears or resentment," he explains. "We get the picture of a spoiled child who does not get what he wants when he wants it."

Dr. Lazowick also tells students at the Berkeley Center for Alcohol Studies that problem drinkers further manifest a tendency toward vague, nonspecific anxiety or chronic fearfulness, which sometimes borders on panic. He may attempt to counteract this anxiety by trying to impress people with his own goodness or commitment to others. "But," says Dr. Lazowick somewhat sadly, "I have never met an alcoholic who has gotten a Christmas card from someone he met in a barroom."

The Berkeley lecturer has also found that alcoholics generally betray a sense of worthlessness. This was the case with Don whose father died when he was seven-years-old. He turned to drink to ease the pain of childhood abandonment. "I'm no good," he rationalized. "Even my father deserted me." It was only under skillful therapy that he came to see that earlier childhood experiences proved that his dad really loved him. When he accepted the fact that he was not responsible for his father's death, Don no longer needed booze to support a sagging ego.

Lazowick's experience has further convinced him that alcoholics are either dependent or counterdependent. "Sixty percent of my alcoholic patients are dependent and demanding," he says. "They frequently say, 'I can't,' which really means, 'I won't.' The other forty percent are counterdependent. They say, 'I've lifted myself up by my own bootstraps. I don't need anyone.' They are all right," says Lazowick, "until you lean on them."

The California psychologist shares the belief of most experts that the two primary defenses of the alcoholic are *denial* and *projection*. "By denial," he explains, "we mean that the problem drinker often denies that he has a problem until long after it is painfully noticeable to other people."

Before he comes to his senses, says Lazowick, the alcoholic will often project what he hates about himself on to his spouse, his boss, and others who figure prominently in his life. "If you want to know about Peter," he suggests, "listen to what he says about Paul. If a man tells you about his parents, his siblings, his wife and his children, you've gotten his complete life story."

Lazowick cringes at the mistakes well-meaning indi-

143

viduals make in trying to "help" the alcoholic. "If you try to 'help' someone," he says, "you give him the message that he is incompetent to help himself." Here are some of the most glaring examples of inappropriate—and generally unrequested—advice given to those who have lost control over their drinking:

"You drink too much." The fact is that a man cannot drink at all once he has crossed that invisible line between uncontrolled and so-called sociable drinking. Yet this common suggestion implies that all the alcoholic has to do is to cut down. This he cannot do.

"You should be ashamed of yourself." Ironically, those who offer this trite moralism would never think of telling the cancer victim or the diabetic that they should likewise be ashamed of their illness. But even if the disease concept is rejected, this pious pronouncement expiates the alcoholic's guilt temporarily and thereby gives him another excuse to drink some more.

"Try these tranquilizers." This commonly-accepted medical practice may ease the burden of many physicians; but it also gives the alcoholic the opportunity to *eat* his booze. Invariably he will use pills in the same way he uses alcohol. If one pill makes him feel good, two will make him feel even better. Consequently, many problem drinkers become cross-addicted and some even end up on a slab in the county morgue. Tranquilizers and sedatives may have a beneficial role to play during withdrawal; but, as Ruth Fox warns, "they are *highly addictive,* and alcoholics need to learn to live without *any* mood-changing chemical." What they don't need is any reinforcement of the notion that they're sick, a message which is implied by the doctor's dictum, "Take this pill."

Lazowick also recommends that alcoholics avoid a one-to-one relationship with a therapist or submit to long-term hospitalization, except in unusual situations. He shares the viewpoint of many experts that problem drinkers do better in a group setting in which others share his problem. The caution against long-term hospitalization is based in part upon the belief that the alcoholic must learn to live without booze in the environment from whence he came. Any treatment which merely heightens his dependency needs is self-defeating.

All therapy—including that of A.A.—must be directed to the alcoholic's tendency toward

Anxiety in interpersonal relationships.

Low tolerance toward frustration and pain.

Ambivalence toward authority.

Feelings of isolation.

Low self-esteem.

Emotional immaturity.

Grandiosity.

Perfectionism.

Compulsiveness.

Guilt and remorse.

But, again, care must be taken not to confuse the chicken with the egg. For, as Howard Clinebell suggests, these characteristics are not entirely the result of prolonged excessive drinking. "This is indicated by the fact," he says, "that the attributes persist in diminished form long after sobriety has been achieved." On the other hand, Father James Royce, speaking as a psychologist, insists that an overwhelming majority of alcoholics began drinking for the same reason as other people. "Until you free the individual from the alcohol," he argues, "you can't tell whether he needs psychiatric help. It may hurt him—rather than help him—if you poke into his Oedipal roots."

Father Royce is one of a growing number of psychologists who break with Freud on the matter of linking alcoholism to a regression in psychosexual development. He, rather, considers the discovery that much behavior is learned or acquired, to be one of the most valuable contributions of modern psychology.

"People are born with deformed legs—but not with inadequate personalities," he argues. "These are developed as a result of life experiences, the buffeting their ego has taken, and the pitifully inadequate ways of coping into which they have inadvertently fallen."

Royce contends that there are many sociocultural pressures facing people today which cannot help but turn them into alcoholics. He specifically cites the military's so-called "happy hour" and the Washington cocktail party. "Many people do not drink for deep-seated psychological reasons," he concludes, "but merely because they are pushed into it."

There are scores of A.A. members who would go along with Father Royce's observations in this regard. Take the case of one happy-go-lucky chap, for example, who drank heavily at home and on the job each day until booze contributed to a near fatal heart attack. He was understandably shaken by this brush with death and pledged that he would never drink again—until fellow workers called their popular colleague from a gin mill and asked him when he would be rejoining the daily festivities. For alcoholics facing these kinds of peer pressures, A.A. says: "If your buddies make you drink, get new friends. Or let them know you're allergic to alcohol!"

Other so-called "normal" people get hooked on booze for other reasons. "Like every other 'social drinker,'" says one AAer, "I knew that there were alcoholics, but I also 'knew' I would never be one. I had more sense than that, and certainly more willpower.

"Suddenly," he continues, "I found myself caught in that downward spiral. No, I told myself, it is not happening to me. This is temporary. I've got problems that will go away. I'll go 'on the wagon' to prove it. I did, first for a month, once for two months. But only another alcoholic can really understand how miserable being 'dry' can be without true sobriety."

Even if Father Royce is correct, there is no question that alcoholism seems to flourish in certain cultures and in certain types of family constellations. For example, the illness is sometimes facetiously called "the Irish virus" because of the high incidence of alcoholism among those of Irish extraction. "You don't have to be Irish," A.A. members often quip, "but it helps." The British, Scandinavians and Russians aren't too far behind!

Similarly, numerous studies have pointed to a correlation between a rigid childhood and excessive drinking in later life. Still another factor seems to be the dominant influence of the parent and/or siblings of the opposite sex. For example, Dr. Albert Ullman, a Tufts University psychologist, found a higher rate of alcoholism in women who identify more closely with their fathers or older brothers than in those who are closer to their mothers. The same thing holds true for boys who are raised under so-called "petticoat government."

The crucial role of the mother in the evolution of the alcoholic was brought home one night at a closed A.A. meeting (for alcoholics only) just before Mother's Day. At such meetings, members are often invited to unburden themselves of matters that are bugging them. "How," asked one man, "do you get through Mother's Day without a drink?"

With that question, the emotional garbage began to flow in torrents. The chairman himself, a professional man, acidly revealed that he couldn't care less if his mother lived or died. Others added to the charged atmosphere by telling their own tragic tales of maternal deprivation and misunderstanding. The climate cooled only after one timid soul gingerly inquired: "But what if you don't hate your mother?"

Toni, a French-speaking newshen, had every reason to feel less than kindly to the woman who gave her birth.

Her mother, an official in the French government, had given her everything that money could buy. She was given the finest clothes and sent to only the best schools. But her most vivid childhood memory is that of returning from boarding school one summer and being told by her mother, "Don't unpack your bags, ma cherie, because I'm sending you to a lovely camp in the mountains."

Toni never knew what it was like to have a father; and her mother pressed ever onward and upward in government circles, neglecting to give her brilliant but extremely sensitive daughter even a semblance of affection and love. Consequently, Toni entered into a long affair with a married newsman after she had gained a reputation of her own in the Fourth Estate. When he died unexpectedly, she turned to alcohol to ease the pain. Toni never took a social drink and seldom drew a sober breath from that moment until her first hospitalization for acute alcoholism. Yet her confused condition did not prevent her from hearing her dying mother scream: "I never want to see my drunken daughter again." It is still doubtful if Toni will ever accept the A.A. program. She can't even accept herself!

Kenneth, on the other hand, was blessed with an "angel" for a mother. The only trouble is that she committed suicide when he was a teenager. And Kenneth blames himself for her tragic death. "If only I had not overslept," he says sadly, "on the morning she jumped out of the window."

There had been several warnings that Kenneth's mother needed hospital care. On one occasion, his sick and elderly father told him to go out and try to find his mother. In his search, a neighborhood patrolman informed him that the poor soul had been taken to the stationhouse. She was later transferred to the municipal mental hospital, where, says Kenneth, "they kept my angel mother like an animal in a cage."

Kenneth is one of the lucky ones. He has come to face the ambivalence of his feelings toward his mother. He still reveres her memory; but he has also become aware of unconscious conflict because she abandoned him just when he needed her most. And he has further discovered that booze is no remedy for psychic pain. Thanks to A.A., he has found that drinking only intensifies his problems.

Benny's story of maternal neglect and deprivation is just as tragic. He was born out of wedlock to a prostitute who showed more affection for her Johns than for her own little boy. He was in the way, and his mother let him know it in no uncertain terms. So Benny turned to burglary and booze as a way of life. He'll tell you that he found more affection in prison than in his own home. Even though it was homosexual in nature.

It is not difficult to understand why Benny would turn against women and seek male companionship. But what is surprising is that tough hardhats and other ex-cons fully accept him within the A.A. fellowship. "I don't dig his style," says tough Tony. "But I have to give him credit that he's staying away from that first drink." If God can speak out of the mouths of children, is it just possible that He can also make His will known through a bunch of recovering drunks?

The role of the alcoholic's wife is no less crucial than that of his mother. "Behind every drunk there stands a dragon," declares the Rev. Kenneth M. Gearhart, an Episcopal priest and director of the Henry Ohlhoff House in San Francisco. "The drunk says to the woman of his dreams, 'I have a bare back,' and she replies, 'I have a big whip.'"

While the wives of a lot of alcoholics would probably like to dig their claws into the bare back of Ken Gearhart, most experts would undoubtedly agree with his thesis—if not his choice metaphors—that problem drinkers often turn to certain types of personalities for lifetime mates. For example, G. M. Price, in a study of the wives of twenty alcoholics, found many of them to be nervous, hostile, basically dependent people, although outwardly they appeared adequate.

Another clinical study indicated that the spouse, because of her own needs, unconsciously seems to encourage her husband's drinking. When he achieves any degree of sobriety, the study disclosed, she herself may show signs of neurotic disturbance.

One of the most engaging articles on the subject was written by Thelma Whalen, who observed four types of wives in her work as an executive in a family service agency. In this position, she writes, she repeatedly ran into Suffering Susan, Controlling Catherine, Wavering Winnifred, and Punitive Polly.

Suffering Susan is the gal who needs to punish herself. This need is gratified by meeting the needs and demands of an alcoholic spouse.

Controlling Catherine is distrustful of men in general and of her drunken husband in particular. She believes that she is more capable of making decisions—perhaps to the point of even picking out her husband's underwear. She wants to control every situation.

Wavering Winnifred is characterized by her need to be needed. She will often go to extreme lengths to sabotage her husband's sobriety because a sudden flush of masculine independence sabotages her own unconscious needs.

Punitive Polly can stand only men who are vulnerable. Her relationship to her alcoholic husband has been described as that of a boa constrictor to a rabbit. She is the eternal club or career woman whose unconscious ego needs are met through rivalry and competition. Her alcoholic husband soon discovers that he's just no match for his wife's invidious drive.

A classic example of the psychogenic character of

many alcoholic marriages is represented by the case of Theresa, who finally left her husband because of his uncontrolled drinking and sexual impotence.

What is clinically interesting about Theresa is that her alcoholic father committed suicide shortly after her birth. Terry's mother and stepfather also showed signs of serious drinking problems. Her childhood was further marred by her stepfather's becoming sexually abusive toward her while she was a little girl. Yet she sought out and married a man who had a problem which had caused her so much tragedy in the past!

Under skillful counseling, Terry has confided that she is sexually frigid. She has further conceded that she might well be a contributing factor to her husband's alcoholism. At present, professional counseling is being supported by Terry's active participation in an Alanon Family Group, an A.A.-oriented fellowship for the husbands and wives of alcoholics. But much more work needs to be done in this case.

Not all cases are as dramatic as that of Terry. There are untold instances in which a shining bride awakens from her honeymoon to discover that the man of her dreams has a serious problem with alcohol. But Joan K. Jackson has shown that the "innocent" spouse can be, and generally is, drawn into the vicious web of cause and effect. Dr. Jackson has delineated seven stages in family adjustment to an alcoholic member:

STAGE ONE: Sporadic incidents of excessive drinking occur, placing a strain on the marriage relationship. In attempts to minimize the drinking, other problems of marital adjustment may be avoided.

STAGE TWO: Social isolation of the family begins as incidents of excessive drinking multiply. Marital thought and behavior becomes drink-centered as tensions rise and the spouse begins to feel self-pity and a loss of self-confidence. The children may start to show signs of emotional disturbance, even as efforts are made to keep the family intact.

STAGE THREE: Efforts to control the drinking are abandoned as the family behaves in a manner geared to relieve tension rather than achieve long-term goals. There is no longer any attempt made to support the alcoholic spouse in his (her) roles as husband and father (or wife and mother). The nonalcoholic partner begins to worry about his or her own sanity, and the emotional deterioration of the children continues.

STAGE FOUR: The nonalcoholic spouse takes over control of the family and the drinking partner is seen as a recalcitrant child. Pity and strong protective feelings largely replace earlier resentment and hostility. The self-confidence of the nonalcoholic spouse begins to be rebuilt as family stability is sought in a manner which attempts to minimize the disruption caused by uncontrolled drinking.

STAGE FIVE: The nonalcoholic partner may seek a separation if the problems and conflicts surrounding such an action can be resolved.

STAGE SIX: The family is reorganized without the presence of the alcoholic.

STAGE SEVEN: The alcoholic achieves sobriety, and attempts are made to reorganize the family once again, this time in light of the traditional roles. However, these efforts may cause problems of their own.

The dynamics of family living after sobriety has been achieved must be appreciated by the marriage partners. The nonalcoholic may retain the fear for a long time that the drinking partner cannot be trusted to carry out his customary roles and responsibilities. Or the spouse may enjoy the role assumed during the period of uncontrolled drinking and feel deeply resentful of the shift in relationships when total abstinence becomes more than a fleeting reality.

During the period of family disorientation, the alcoholic has very likely been able to provoke the anger and arouse the anxiety of other members of the family. But these emotions only contribute to the progress of the illness. The Rev. Joseph L. Kellermann, director of the Council on Alcoholism, Charlotte, North Carolina, puts it like this:

> The family members must first learn to cope with their own problems before any beneficial effects can reach the alcoholic. This requires help just as any serious illness requires help outside the family. The alcoholic can continue to deny that he has a drinking problem and that he does not need help as long as the family, friends, ministers, doctors, lawyers or employer provide an automatic escape from the consequences of drinking.

Mr. Kellermann, one of the most knowledgeable clergy experts in the field, has developed this thesis in an engaging and highly useful little booklet entitled "Alcoholism—A Merry-Go-Round Named Denial." It should be obtained from the Charlotte Council on Alcoholism for use by the family, friends, employer and pastor of the alcoholic. He has also written another booklet, "A Guide for the Family."

Kellermann views the progress of uncontrolled drinking as a drama in three acts, in which others besides the alcoholic plays supporting and crucial roles. There is always the Enabler, a guilt-ridden Mr. Clean, whose own anxiety and guilt lead him to set up a "rescue mission" to save the alcoholic from the immediate crisis and relieve the unbearable tension created by the situation. There is also the Victim—often the boss or business partner—who assumes responsibility for getting the work done if the alcoholic is absent due to drinking. And, finally, there is always the Provocatice or Compensator, the wife or mother who is the center of the alcoholic home. Her role is that of constantly adjusting to every crisis produced by the illness and compensating for everything that goes wrong within the home or marriage.

"One person cannot become an alcoholic without the help of at least another," says Kellermann flatly. "It cannot appear in isolation, progress in isolation, nor maintain itself in isolation. One person drinks in a way that is completely unlike social drinking. Others react to the drinking and its consequences. The drinker responds to the reaction and drinks again. This sets up a merry-go-round of denial and counterdenial, a downward spiral, which is called alcoholism."

But this does not answer the burning question of what can—and should—be done to break the vicious cycle.

The nonalcoholic spouse must first stop assuming the blame for all that goes wrong in an alcoholic marriage. "The wife is no more responsible for alcoholism than she would be for the existence of diabetes or tuberculosis in her husband," Kellermann insists. "No wife ever made her husband an alcoholic. Therefore no wife can 'unmake' her husband, or be held responsible for the recovery."

At the same time, the North Carolina Alcoholic Rehabilitation Program has compiled a list of Do's and Don't's which may aid in the recovery process:

DO learn the facts about alcoholism.
DO develop an attitude to match the facts.
DO talk to someone who understands alcoholism.
DO take a personal inventory of yourself.
DO go to a clinic or A.A.
DO maintain a healthy atmosphere in your home.
DO encourage your husband's (or wife's) new interests.
DO take a relapse lightly if there is one.
DO pass on your knowledge of alcoholism to others.
DON'T preach and lecture to the alcoholic.
DON'T have a "holier-than-thou" attitude.
DON'T use the "if you loved me" appeal.
DON'T make threats you won't carry out.
DON'T hide liquor or pour it out.
DON'T argue with the alcoholic during a drunk.
DON'T make an issue over the treatment.
DON'T expect an immediate, 100 percent recovery.

DON'T be jealous of recovery methods.
DON'T try to protect the drinker from alcohol.

If your dad or mom has a serious problem with drinking, there is an organization called Alateen for young people between the ages of thirteen and twenty. It is an outgrowth of Alanon, the worldwide fellowship for relatives and friends of alcoholics. Its purpose is to encourage members in ways in which they can effectively cope with uncontrolled drinking within the family circle.

Alateen teaches that compulsive drinking is a disease, which should no more be condemned than any other illness. It encourages its members to regard the sick patient's loss of dignity with compassion rather than with contempt. At the same time, it seeks to help young people achieve some degree of emotional detachment from the parent's problem. They come to realize—as the alcoholic himself must—that they are powerless over alcohol.

There comes a time during the recovery process when family counseling and/or psychotherapy may be extremely beneficial. However, the first step on that road to recovery might well be personal participation by the non-alcoholic family members in Alanon or Alateen.

And, if you have a drinking problem yourself, why not give yourself a break. Life somehow gets better when you get off the merry-go-round of denial. You just might catch the brass ring with a call to A.A.

Get the booze out of your system before you entertain any more thoughts that you're going crazy or likely to die of some rare and exotic disease you think you might have picked up at Anzio, Midway, or Kaesong. Of course, that's easier said than done. But A.A. knows all about the shakes, the sweats and that craving for another drink. We've all been through it ourselves—and we've discovered that the vicious chain can be broken by staying away from one drink one day—or even one hour—at a time.

If you still feel you need professional help after a

reasonable period of sobriety, there are generally several avenues open to you. The National Council on Alcoholism, with affiliates in major cities across the country, is one source of information. They will know all about out-patient facilities and other private and public services available in or near your community. They'll also be able to make suggestions regarding detoxification for seriously ill alcoholics.

Community mental health agencies can advise individuals and families as to available counseling programs. Some families may find that sobriety does not mean serenity—that new problems have popped up after the parent or spouse has quit drinking. If this is the case, don't leave the answer to laymen. Get professional advice.

Dr. O. Quentin Hyder, a devout Presbyterian layman and author of *The Christian's Handbook of Psychiatry,* has stressed that psychotherapy has undergone change since World War II. He himself has largely abandoned Freudian techniques for those of the "reality therapy" of William Glasser.

"The important thing is to find a therapist who is efficient, even though he may not be a Christian," says Dr. Hyder. "The patient and the therapist should give one another a reasonable amount of time—say three months. Then the future course can be reevaluated at that time."

Two final words of advice: Don't expect miracles from a therapist after only a few sessions. And let your pastor know of your decision to join A.A. It will be like music to his ears and joy to his heart!

7

Whence Cometh My Help?

"Wherefore seeing we also are compassed about with so great a cloud of witnesses, let us lay aside every weight, and the sin which doth so easily beset us, and let us run with patience the race that is set before us, Looking unto Jesus the author and finisher of our faith; who for the joy that was set before him endured the cross, despising the shame, and is set down at the right hand of the throne of God" (Hebrews 12: 1, 2).

THE TELEPHONE rang.

It was the emergency room of the hospital calling to let a panic-stricken mother know that her nine-year-old son had suffered severe facial cuts in the playground of his school.

Tears streamed down the handsome little face when the distraught woman arrived on the scene. Her son wasn't crying because of shock or physical pain. He rather plaintively asked, "Mommy, how are we going to pay for this?"

It was a good question because both mother and son knew only too well that most of the family's limited resources went to buy Daddy's booze. But this long-suffering woman gently patted away the tears and told the little boy not to worry, as the surgeon's skillful hand sutured the deep lacerations.

Then the light dawned. "Don't you remember," the mother asked almost jubilantly. "We paid for that school accident policy. I'll bet they will take care of this."

That made the lad feel much better.

The wounds quickly healed, leaving only the faintest trace of a scar. The insurance company was also prompt in settling the claim. But it made a gigantic mistake. It sent the check in the name of the alcoholic father.

"I knew that the doctor deserved every penny for the wonderful job he did on my son's face," the man admitted to A.A. friends years later. "But I also knew that I desperately needed that money for drink."

The surgeon sent his bill each month in an effort to get paid for services rendered, while the insurance company itself inquired as to whether the check had been lost in the mail. But all inquiries went unanswered. Finally they stopped.

"But the dark memory of that misspent check haunted me right to the door of A.A.," says this sober father now. "I felt like a criminal who had escaped punishment. Then again, I was my own punishment because I had to live with myself."

This typical experience of a recovering alcoholic makes it difficult to accept the somewhat rigid stand of a nationally known clergyman who thinks that "sentimental do-gooders" coddle problem drinkers too much.

This highly respected pastor, a man with an enviable reputation in evangelism and world missions, is probably right when he suggests that the alcoholic is like a baby who organizes his whole life around a bottle. But his recommended "cure" is less convincing.

The alcoholic "is as dependent on a bottle as the newborn in a maternity ward," he says. "And he requires as much nursing. He doesn't need sympathy . . . he needs a spanking! He needs the whine knocked out of him."

It is true that the compulsive drinker does not need sympathy; but he does need someone who understands both him and his problem. At the expense of a poor pun, he'll keep right on *whining* until he gives up *wining*.

Drinking is his response for all of the "spankings" he has received in life. Punitive treatment may occasionally have some beneficial effect. But often as not threats and penalties merely expiate his crushing guilt and remorse and give him one more good excuse to defiantly lift his glass in protest against a world he believes has treated him cruelly.

The fear of the *law* did nothing to make that alcoholic father sober up and pay those bills that were rightfully due. He only began to meet his personal responsibilities after he had been apprehended by *grace* and learned within the A.A. fellowship that recovery involves making amends to those who have been hurt by prolonged drunken behavior.

It has always been a source of wonder that so many who claim the Gospel of grace for themselves expect others to live under bondage to the false gospel of salvation by good works. Paul Tournier, the beloved Christian psychiatrist, has observed that all churches are composed of those "who are of a moralistic nature, censorious and showing morbid guilt," while others are "generous spirited people, messengers of a God who pardons, who themselves alleviate guilt."

While both groups can glean from the Bible passages which support their attitude, says Tournier, people unfortunately "pick out precisely those passages . . . which are not addressed to them!

"Psychologists ought to show the churches clearly that this is the case," he writes. "It is a daily observation with them, and it is the source of numerous catastrophes.

Those who flaunt their self-satisfaction, at the cost of a repression of their guilt, who scorn and pass judgment upon other people and flatter themselves on their virtues, are the ones who notice the assurance of grace which really concerns the people they condemn; while the latter worry themselves by reading the divine warnings which are really directed to the former."

Something is terribly wrong with our concept of the Gospel when clinical studies have indicated that alcoholism often flourishes among children of church members. P. M. Sessions, a psychiatric social worker, has laid the blame for this tragic phenomenon on the fact that *superego* religion has too often been emphasized at the expense of *ego*-building faith. Mr. Sessions defines "superego religion" as that in which tradition and authority prevail, and in which the individual's self-punitive tendencies are magnified. "Ego religion," on the other hand, emphasizes a person's trusting relationship to a loving God. It is this kind of faith, says Sessions, which is so often sorely lacking in the lives of so many alcoholics. None of them have ever been saved from themselves by a good spanking!

The testimony of countless recovering alcoholics, inside A.A. and out, seems to indicate that the God of their childhood was a god of wrath whose anger had to be constantly appeased. In time, the fear and guilt produced by such rigid dogmatism drove these unfortunate people to the bottle in their effort to find relief from psychic and spiritual pain. Finding no balm in Gilead, they sought a balm in booze!

Paul Tillich, while enjoying less than enthusiastic support in evangelical circles, may be closer to the spirit of the Gospel than many of his detractors in his analysis of what he calls the conflict between autonomy and heteronomy. These terms might sound like so much theological jargon; but they actually put the finger on the religious experience of so many alcoholics.

At the risk of oversimplification, Tillich says that people often grow up under bondage to a set of laws (heteronomous) which are imposed from without and which stifle their own personal development. In time, he contends, many individuals rebel against this outside authority and become autonomous, or a law unto themselves. It takes the miracle of grace to make the New Man—the person whose behavior is guided by a law from within. Tillich calls this internalized rule for daily living the theonomous law. "It is an effect of the final revelation," he says, "which no autonomy can produce and which no heteronomy can prevent." It is validated by the light and love of God.

Dwight L. Moody, the great American evangelist, tells a story which is much to the point. He had been preaching one night and had invited members of the congregation to remain behind if they had any questions of a spiritual nature on their minds. But the audience left the church quickly after the service, and Moody was about to put on his hat and coat when he suddenly spotted a man huddled behind the furnace. "He had no coat," says Moody, "and he was weeping bitterly."

His story was that of thousands who have hit the skids. He had lost his family and had squandered $20,000 in drink in the course of just a few months. "I have drunk up the coat off my back," he said. "And if there is hope for a poor sinner like me, I'd like to be saved."

"It was just like a cup of refreshment to talk to that man," the great evangelist said later. "I did not dare give him any money for fear he would drink it up. But I got him a place to stay that night, took an interest in him, and got him a coat.

"Six months after that when I left Chicago for Europe," Moody added, "that man was one of the most earnest Christian men I knew. The Lord has blessed him wonderfully. He was an active, capable man."

This story tells us as much about the greatness of Dwight L. Moody as it does about the man whose life had been reclaimed by the power of a miracle-working God. Mr. Moody certainly did not suggest for a minute that the poor fellow should just cut down on his drinking and "learn to drink like a man." But neither did he give him a verbal "spanking" by quoting a few well-chosen Scripture texts which would only increase his sense of guilt and despair. Rather, he identified with the man and accepted him where he was. It was his ability to show loving concern for the least of Christ's brethren that demonstrated far more eloquently than words that the redemptive grace of God was sufficient to meet the deepest needs of a man (II Corinthians 12: 9).

If psychotherapy has anything to teach the Christian community, it should be the fact that judgment belongs only to God. "It is through fear of being judged," says Paul Tournier, "that so many people today go to the doctor or the psychotherapist rather than to the clergyman. Rightly or wrongly, they invest the parson with a spirit of judgment which they fear. . . . The doctor seems more neutral, just because he does not meddle with morality. He tries to understand a man's behavior as an astronomer strives to understand that of the stars or why an eclipse takes place."

However, Dr. Tournier hastens to add that psychotherapy's "virtue of nonjudgment" may be more of a myth than a reality. "We see in it a sign of God's grace," he says. "We can be proud of it. But is it not just at the moment when we are flattering ourselves about some virtue that we most run the risk of blinding ourselves to the times when we are unfaithful to that very virtue? No one, I think, is more subtly exposed than we psychotherapists to the repression of judgment into the unconscious, and just because we attach so much importance to showing ourselves as uncritical of our patients."

Somehow Dr. Tournier's candid comment about the unconscious shortcomings of his own craft again recall the wisdom of Herman Kregel: "A boy Scout with love in his heart can do more for the recovering alcoholic than the most brilliant psychiatrist who hates the guts of the alcoholic."

But Dr. Kregel might well have included a lot of self-satisfied saints in his rather scathing rebuke.

Sam Shoemaker sought to demonstrate the spiritual potential of the recovered alcoholic in that memorable sermon mentioned earlier, "What the Church Can Learn From Alcoholics Anonymous." He took for his text: "God chose what is foolish in the world to shame the wise, God chose what is weak in the world to shame the strong . . ." (I Corinthians 1: 27 RSV).

Suggesting that the Church could be "reawakened and revitalized by those insights and practices found in A.A.," Dr. Sam observed: "I think some of you may be a little horrified at this suggestion. I fear you will be saying to yourself, 'What have we, who have always been decent people, to learn from a lot of reconstructed drunks?' And perhaps you may thereby reveal to yourself how very far you are from the spirit of Christ and the Gospel, and how very much in need of precisely the kind of check-up that may come to us from A.A." Here is what Dr. Shoemaker found the Church could learn from Alcoholics Anonymous:

. . . Nobody gets anywhere till he recognizes a clearly defined need. These people do not come to A.A. to get made a little better. They do not come because the best people are doing it. They come because they are desperate.

. . . Men are redeemed in a life-changing fellowship. Alcoholics Anonymous does not expect to let anybody who comes in stay as he is. They know he is in need and must have help. They live for nothing else but to extend and keep extending that help.

... (There is) the necessity for definite personal dealing with people ... I've heard (AAs) laboring with one another, now patient as a mother, now savage as a prizefighter, now careful in explanation, now pounding in a heavy personal challenge, but always knowing the desperate need and the sure answer. Are we in the Church like that?

... (There) is the necessity for a real change of heart, a true conversion. As we come Sunday after Sunday, year after year, we are supposed to be in a process of transformation. Are we? The AAs are.

One deeply evangelical facility with an effective A.A. oriented ministry for alcoholics is the Calvary Rehabilitation Center, an affiliate of the Christian Reformed Church in Phoenix, Arizona. Its chaplain, the Rev. Ralph Heynen, has noted that, while alcohol and drugs are the most obvious means of escape, work and tv "addicts" also show the strains of the "anxiety of a splintered life." The antidote in every case, he says, is "the most powerful human force in the world—love."

Lou Austin, a lively octogenarian, has emphasized that no one has the right to judge another human being. "You learn that almost everyone is an 'alcoholic' of a sort—one whose desires in a certain direction have gone out of bounds," he writes. "There is the money 'alcoholic,' the sex 'alcoholic,' the power 'alcoholic,' the publicity 'alcoholic,' the eating 'alcoholic.' "

Alcoholics Anonymous has done such a magnificent job because each member *knows* that he of himself is powerless, that God alone can help him," Mr. Austin observes. "Why should 'alcoholics' of another sort feel so respectable and look down upon the liquor alcoholic? Every sincere member of A.A. lives the partnership life and carries with him the presence of God. Is that not the answer to all forms of 'alcoholism'?"

Friends claim that Lou Austin looks younger today than he did thirty-five years ago. His prescription for a happy life?

"Breathe out ego," he advises. "And breathe in God."

Paul Tournier himself is a living example of what this kind of "medicine" can do for the anxiety-prone, guilt-ridden spirit of man. His own childhood could hardly be called ideal. He was an orphan who grew up "sensitive to the shame of poverty." "I felt ashamed and guilty," he writes, "at not being like the others." Yet he grew up to become the most beloved Christian psychiatrist in the world today. He found himself when he found Jesus Christ.

"Spiritual medicine does not set out to give moral uplift to the sick instead of treating them," he says. "It is the most scientific medicine possible, applied by doctors who are strict with themselves, and who rely on the grace of God. The doctor who has experienced in his own life the effects of grace knows that, without excluding medicines, advice, and psychological analyses, grace is more precious than all these. He looks upon all these means of treatment as given to him by the grace of God.

"But," he adds emphatically, "he knows that more important than all these gifts is the gift of grace itself—the awareness of fellowship with the person of Jesus Christ, who suddenly, often at the moment when he is least expected, breaks into a person's life and transforms it, even if it remains bowed under the weight of suffering."

Consequently, Dr. Tournier is unsympathetic with clergymen who routinely buttonhole the distressed and oppressed with the question, "Are you saved?" The task is rather to identify with the person in his discomfort, he suggests, and seek to be a channel of the grace of a loving God. When grace has been apprehended, the Christian can then offer the name of the Great Physician!

The works of Paul Tournier—*The Meaning of Persons,*

Guilt and Grace, The Person Reborn—read like ongoing chapters of a continuing Pentecost. Like his apostolic namesake, he is a rugged champion of the miracle-working power of grace. He is forever demonstrating how the "works of the law" only lead an individual into a deeper sense of bondage.

There is, for example, the touching story of his wife as they sat together at the dinner table. "I asked (her)," he writes, "why her face suddenly lit up with a strange smile.

" 'Look,' she said, 'I had to cut into the butter at one end and you cut into it at the other end. I just thought of what would have been said if that had been done as a child: a well-brought-up child should continue to take the butter from the end already begun. Your action was like a blow for freedom!' "

There is another story in the same vein about two men who found Christ at a Bible conference abroad. One threw his package of cigarettes into a lake to show that he had been freed of the nicotine habit. The other did just the opposite. He had been told throughout his boyhood that tobacco was evil. So he asked a friend for a cigarette, lit it, and cheerfully puffed away to demonstrate his new-found liberty as a Christian!

In his work among alcoholics, Dr. Tournier attributes the success of A.A. and other organizations to a recognition that the *whole person* must be restored to health. "Alcoholism is not . . . a primary problem," he believes, "but a secondary one, a flight, a compensation for secret distress. This is why it rarely gives way before moral exhortation."

To support this claim, Dr. Tournier cites the case of a young woman who had come to see him about a problem. "As a governess in America," he says, "she had taken a doctor's advice to drink port 'to pep her up' while convalescing from a slight illness. This inclination toward drinking had gone on growing until it had become a slavery from which she could not tear herself.

"What interested me," he writes, "was not the drink problem in itself, but the reason for which she had taken to drink. There are many people who take a little alcoholic drink during convalescence and yet do not become alcoholics as a result."

Dr. Tournier met with the young woman twice. He felt discouraged that nothing had been accomplished about the drinking problem. But, in the middle of the third visit, he felt constrained to ask her to join him in silent prayer. "In the silence," he says, "an idea came very vividly into my mind: her mother. The subject had never been mentioned in our conversations. I said to her: 'Your mother.' She seemed most surprised, and said that her mother was a saintly woman, against whom she had no complaint at all. That was all: She went. I was disappointed.

"But that same evening," Dr. Tournier continues, "I had a telephone call from her. 'That's it!' she said, and to my astonishment went on. 'It was while I was going down the stairs from your apartment that suddenly the light broke in on me, as if a veil had been torn away.

" 'I saw that I have always borne a grudge against my mother for being a saintly woman, she continued, because her saintliness put me to shame. I saw that I had become a governess in order to have a chance to go abroad and get far away from her example, because it hurt me to have her near me. Over there in America the Atlantic Ocean was not enough to separate me from my mother, and unconsciously I dug a moral ditch between her and me by means of drink . . .' "

This story reflects something far deeper than unconscious causes in personality development. It is rather the story of guilt being overcome by grace. The girl became reconciled to her mother, and, according to Dr. Tournier, her drinking immediately ceased.

It further points up the fact that there is a judgmental attitude—not without a morality of its own—that can be constructively used in the treatment of alcoholics. "The nonmoralistic, nonrejecting judgmental attitude has the elements of understanding and acceptance," says John Keller, "and moves in the direction of helping a person to greater self-awareness and greater honesty about himself and his condition and his responsibility. It is basic in the process of confrontation."

In this case, a Christian psychiatrist was moved by prayer to put his finger on the root cause of the young woman's excessive drinking—her mother, (which was not true in my case). His technique hardly represented orthodox analytical methods; but it was eminently productive.

Many evangelical clergymen with clinical training would now agree that it is possible to accept the legitimate insights of Sigmund Freud and his successors without accepting their bias against Christian faith. "When Freud is talking about how to cure neurotics," says C. S. Lewis, "he is speaking as a specialist on his own subject; but when he goes on to talk general philosophy, he is speaking as an amateur. . . .

"But psychoanalysis itself, apart from all the philosophical additions that Freud and others have made to it," Lewis adds, "is not in the least contradictory to Christianity. Its technique overlaps with Christian morality at some points, and it would not be a bad thing if every person knew something about it. But it does not run the same course all the way; for the two techniques are doing rather different things."

Father James Royce would agree with this position. "Psychology cannot provide religious truths," he says. "But perhaps it can facilitate the communication of them by helping the pastor to understand persons.

"People want desperately to be accepted, loved, respected—to feel important, to be somebody," he notes.

"They want to know that they can count on somebody or something. They want security and trust. They want absolute confidential secrecy regarding what they tell us. They want to be thought of as generous and kind, not mean and small. They want to cooperate, to belong to the group, but they are often so inept and fearful that they disguise this with an air of disdain or contempt for the cooperative venture."

However, there is little doubt that alcoholism *does* seem to hit many people who otherwise appear reasonably content and worry-free. One happy-go-lucky chap, for example, had conned his adoring wife into believing that he only had "a few short ones with the boys" until his excessive drinking contributed to a serious heart attack. It was only then that the little woman found eight bottles of "the hard stuff" hidden all over the house.

It all goes back to that matter of the chicken and the egg. The illness itself is extremely complex; and so are its victims. For that reason, many experts will cite numerous cases to support their contention that alcoholism is merely symptomatic of a much deeper psychological disturbance, while others are just as adamant that alcoholism results from prolonged excessive drinking. Alcoholics Anonymous itself, not wishing to become involved in such arguments, simply suggests that "some people are sicker than others."

While alcoholism has proved to be a fertile field for psychological research, it can also become a meeting place for theological understanding. Christian leaders of various traditions have discovered that they can share— and deepen—the winsome faith of so many recovered alcoholics without sacrificing their own integrity in spiritual matters.

However, Paul Tournier raises the uncomfortable question as to whether churchmen themselves have not often contributed to much of the emotional trauma which cuts across sectarian lines. "I see so many people torn in two between Catholicism and Protestantism," he observes. "The more priests and pastors they consult, each denouncing the errors of the other's church, the more are they pushed into opposing the one to the other in their minds, thus sterilizing their spiritual life; and so the unity of the Church, which Christ commanded, is in spirit destroyed.

"Moreover," he continues, "many people are torn in two by the dichotomy between the doctrines of some sect or religious movement to which they have been attracted by its fervor, and those of the traditional Church which denounces its errors but lacks its zeal."

Dr. Tournier has warned that the partisan spirit only "impoverishes the mind." "Behind every system of thought there is a living experience," he insists. ". . . (Yet) how many upholders of orthodoxy seem to have fossilized minds, through having lost that unquenchable disquiet and curiosity which are the precondition of every advance in the spiritual life.

"Every discord between form and substance, between what others see and the reality of the heart, is a denial of the Gospel and can only be a source of psychological trouble," he contends. " 'Being a Christian,' Zwingli used to say, 'is not chatting about Christ, but living as He lived.' "

It is amazing to see how A.A. has made "true believers" out of those churchmen of various backgrounds who have taken time to get to know the program and members of the fellowship. In the early days, there was Sam Shoemaker, an evangelical, who rubbed shoulders at A.A. get-togethers with Father Ed Dowling, a Jesuit, and the incomparable Sister Ignatia, a nursing nun. This truly ecumenical spirit has remained down to this day. It has been marked by integrity to one's own doctrinal standards, as well as by an almost evangelical fervor in defense of certain basic Christian beliefs.

Churchmen like Jim Royce often sound like recovered alcoholics themselves in their praise of A.A.'s spiritual program. "Some people criticize A.A. for being too emotional," he quips. "But these people have been brought back from hell. It's no disgrace to admit that we are dependent on the One who created the galaxies of the universe.

"Some say they don't want to depend upon God because it's a crutch," he continues. "Do you depend upon oxygen? Then admit it. This isn't a crutch. It's a reality."

The priest's enthusiasm is matched by that of a close A.A. friend, Jim T., a Catholic layman and a retired machinist. Listen to the story he wrote down expressly for this book:

"My early days in the program were filled with awe and wonder. I was deeply in awe of all of the goodness that I could see about me—the happy, contented people, the beautiful concern they had for me and mine. My attitude changed from darkest despair to the greatest elation. All this with no apparent effort on my part. They told me that I was enjoying the 'miracle of A.A.'

"I had no concept of a Higher Power or God. I'm sure I wanted one; but I was confused about what I thought to be an Abstract Being.

"One day at work, I had a tray of work that had to be cylindrically ground. The work pieces were one-half inch diameter shafts, about three inches long, and, at each end of the shaft, a center bearing hole had been drilled. I was to grind the outside diameter of these shafts true to the centers.

"That's when it dawned upon me that every part that we made had to be true to itself. If it wasn't, it was scrapped out. Only those parts that were true could be used in a final assembly.

"I needed a center. I needed to be true to that center. It didn't matter that I suspected that others around me were not true to that center. My immediate concern was myself. That day brought me the first of many subsequent and beautiful spiritual awakenings."

The story of the Master's encounter with the woman taken in adultery has much to say not only to the alcoholic but also to his accusers. It is also a classic example of the relationship between psychology and the Gospel.

This woman had been charged with a capital crime. For the Mosaic law decreed that anyone convicted of adultery should be put to death (Leviticus 20: 10; Deuteronomy 22: 13-24). The *Mishnah,* or codified law of Judaism, went even further by prescribing death by strangulation for the man and stoning for the woman involved.

One of the first recorded references to drunkenness in the Bible decrees the same severe punishment for the compulsive drinker. The parents themselves were required to bring the offender before the elders of the city and publicly declare: "This our son is a glutton and a drunkard." "And," says the Bible, "all the men of his city shall stone him with stones, that he die" (Deuteronomy 21: 21).

Such texts indicate that drunkenness was no less reprehensible than adultery to ancient Judaism. In the one instance, the rabbis declared that "every Jew must die before he will commit idolatry, murder or adultery." In the other, it was said that "to be a drunkard is to cease being a Jew."

Actually, Judaism has traditionally identified the sin of excessive drinking with that of idolatry. One writer has gone so far as to suggest that the particular sin of the compulsive drinker is his symbolic alliance with Satan, a pact with or possession by the bad father. "He seeks power, protection, and pleasure beyond other people," says this observer. "He fights against the restrictive Good Father. He must renounce the Lord and turn to Satan.

172

After his ordeal with Satan, the alcoholic is left helpless, an inferior sinner with Satan's mark on him."

This same theme is central to an ancient Hebrew legend concerning the nature of alcohol addiction. One day, while Noah was plowing a field, the Devil approached and asked what he was doing. "I am planting a vineyard," Noah replied. "When the fruit is ripe, the grapes are excellent to eat, either moist or dried, and when pressed the juices become wine which warms the body and the spirit."

The Devil suggested that they become partners in the vineyard and Noah agreed. Thereupon the Devil killed a sheep, a lion, a monkey, and a pig in such a manner that the blood of each animal flowed around the roots of the vines.

The rabbis interpreted the Devil's action to mean that man is ordinarily like the sheep—mild and inoffensive; after he starts to drink, he feels like the lion—proud and confident of his strength; if he continues to drink in excess, he starts to chatter aimlessly and scampers about like the foolish monkey; and if he drinks still more, he falls to the ground and wallows in the filth like the pig.

Not a bad description of the man or woman who has been caught in the deathlike grip of uncontrolled drinking.

So many alcoholics remark that they first turned to booze when they came to believe that the God of their childhood had let them down. The amber liquid, on the other hand, made them feel almost in tune with the infinite at the beginning of their drinking careers. "The sway of alcohol over mankind," says psychologist William James, "is unquestionably due to its power to stimulate the mystical faculties of human nature . . . It makes him for the moment one with the truth." It is only after the alcoholic has "hit bottom" that he discovers to his sorrow that Demon Rum is in fact "the god who failed." But the lesson has been learned too late.

While Judaism has always accepted wine as a gift of God to man, it has been intransigent in its condemnation of the abuse of alcoholic beverages. There is little reason to doubt that the religious leaders who confronted Jesus with the sin of adultery would have been just as hard-nosed in their opinion of the problem drinker.

Our Lord Himself certainly would not have condoned the *behavior* of the offender in either case. But neither did He reject the *person* whose life had been marred by sin, guilt and shame. "All that the Father giveth me shall come to me," He declared, "and him that cometh to me I will in no wise cast out" (John 6: 37).

These very words represented the first point of friction between the Galilean and the religious leaders of His day. He spoke with an authority which suggested equality with the Father. It was an inner authority which the scribes and Pharisees did not possess themselves. But its power could not be denied as the spiritually hungry multitudes abandoned the Temple to go up into the mount with the Master.

A second point of friction between Jesus and those ancient ecclesiastics involved the fact that He had an uncanny knack of cutting straight through a man's pretense and hypocrisy. It was all well and good for a bunch of spiritually impotent men to boast that they had never been guilty of adultery. "But," said Jesus, "I say unto you, That whosoever looketh on a woman to lust after her hath committed adultery with her already in his heart" (Matthew 5: 28).

Such words must have burned like a hot iron upon the soul. For none of these self-righteous leaders had ever considered themselves guilty before the law for their fantasies; and yet they were quick to condemn a young woman for acting out her thoughts.

Isn't it strange that our sense of justice is so selective

in its choice of victim? The scribes and Pharisees were quite willing to throw this poor girl to the wolves. Yet they could boast that they were heirs to the promises God made to David—an adulterer and a man who resorted to murder after he had failed to accomplish his sinful purpose by getting his victim drunk!

The same human tendency is often operative when it comes to the attitude of the Christian community toward those with a serious drinking problem. So many are willing to condemn the alcoholic as a weak-willed, spineless sinner. It is only when the illness strikes close to home that their vision is enlarged enough to allow them to admit that compulsive drinking may after all be a disease. And thank God for that!

But the important point is that Jesus looked beyond the letter of the law to its spiritual intent, something self-righteous saints have never been able to do.

While Jesus has always appealed more to sinners than to saints, these scribes and Pharisees were really out to get Him. By confronting Him with the woman taken in adultery, they thought they had also confronted Him with an impossible dilemma. If He said the woman must die, He would lose the devotion of those who considered Him to be a friend of sinners. If, on the other hand, He suggested that the woman should be pardoned, then it could be said that He was teaching men to break the law of Moses and even encouraging them to commit adultery. Many sincere and open-minded followers of Christ have faced a similar dilemma when it comes to the abuse of beverage alcohol.

As always, the Master is the model for Christian action. He made it abundantly clear that only those who are without fault are in a position to judge someone else. In the case of this poor girl, He told her accusers: "He that is without sin among you, let him first cast a stone at her." One by one they silently picked up their skirts and left.

But that was merely a negative response to human need. The scribes and Pharisees left; Jesus stayed behind. So it is that Howard Clinebell has suggested that the churches can perform an effective service to alcoholics and their families if they provide a "climate of Christian acceptance." "Alcoholics," he emphasizes, "are extremely sensitive people who can sense unvoiced criticism. Their only remaining refuge from criticism and rejection is . . . another drink."

However, it is important to note that Christian acceptance involves the *person*—not his *behavior*. Jesus made it indelibly clear to this woman that He did not condone her actions. He neither winked at her sin nor did He excuse her because of a wretched childhood or impoverished social background. He rather made her face up to herself and her problem.

Some might suggest that Jesus employed a technique which today is called reality therapy. He said in effect: "I am not going to pass judgment *now*. You have sinned. Now go and sin no more. And I'll be there to help you." He did not increase her sense of guilt. But neither did He free her from all moral responsibility.

The Rev. John C. Ford, a Jesuit authority on alcoholism, agrees with those who recognize that the drinker's freedom and moral obligations are diminished under the sway of alcohol. "The honest and enlightened testimony of the drinker's own conscience is the best criterion we have of his subjective responsibility," he writes. "In the final analysis, after making allowance for the pathological character of his addiction, judgment must be left to a merciful God." However, Father Ford makes these interesting observations:

"A great many alcoholics begin their drinking by way of harmless self-indulgence, but this indulgence soon becomes so attractive that it leads to sinful excess. Sins of deliberate drunkenness become habitual.

Little by little one moral ideal after another is allowed to grow dim: honesty goes; humility goes; purity goes. There ensue: increasing selfishness and egocentricity; increasing self-deception; increasing neglect of family, business and friends; increasing resentments and cynicism; . . . and, finally, in many cases, a despairing rejection of Almighty God Himself. The lessons learned in childhood are disdained. What began as harmless self-indulgence, degenerates into addiction.

"The alcoholic finds himself morally and spiritually bankrupt, at odds with God, at odds with his own conscience, and finally deprived of his own self-respect."

Thus, as David E. Roberts points out, the motive behind the Christian doctrine of sin "is not to drive in a sense of despair and insufficiency just because one enjoys seeing men wriggle in agony." "The motive behind it," he says, "is to reach full awareness of the depth of the human problem. It is folly to say that we should not feel guilty when we look back on our own lives, leaving nothing out. The sense of guilt is a sign that we have not become totally insensitive, hardened and irrecoverable." It is also a sign that there is hope for recovery!

'Twas grace that taught my heart to fear,
    And grace my fears relieved;
How precious did that grace appear
    The hour I first believed.

Far more is involved here than the mere question of excessive drinking—or sexual promiscuity, for that matter. Christianity rather sees man as a being whose nature was so constituted that it can only maintain its health through personal fellowship with God. Or as St. Augustine put it: "Thou has made us for Thyself; and our hearts are restless until they find their rest in Thee."

When man is alienated from his Maker, the result is sickness of soul, and mind, and sometimes even the body. "Strictly speaking," says Frederick B. Rea, the principal

of Epworth Theological College, Salisbury, Rhodesia, ". . .
there is only one sin in the primary meaning of the word—
namely man's refusal to live a life of fellowship with
God. That is the responsible action of a free person; it is
freely chosen and deliberate. All other sins are secondary
and derivative. They are the effects and consequences of
the primary act, and they are not committed with the
same degree of deliberateness or freedom. They are as
symptoms of the main disease."

Dr. Rea traces the downward path of the alcoholic in
terms of the first chapter of Paul's letter to the saints at
Rome. The first stage comes when men generally reject
their own Creator: "Professing themselves to be wise, they
became fools," and "their foolish heart was darkened."
The second stage is set into motion when a host of "dis-
honorable passions" emerge in the life adrift from God.
Says Dr. Rea:

"With the sealing off of the channel of religious affection towards God, the balance of emotional life is
disturbed and an excess flows into other channels.
A man finds himself committing acts which he knows
to be evil and which, with a part of himself, he ab-
hors and condemns; yet he cannot help himself, for
now he has become a slave of his sin.

"In light of these facts, we begin to have a deeper
understanding of the nature of sin. It is not sufficient
to define it as 'doing what you know to be wrong,'
nor does it suffice to say that an act is free from sin
simply because the agent has acted either in igno-
rance or else under compulsion. Sin is a disease and
man is guilty of contracting it when he first rejects
God."

Actually, all men are in the same boat. For all men
are sinners by fact and by choice. While the alcoholic
may show the effects of his folly to a greater degree, Dr.
Rea points out that our Lord indicated that he may be no
more sinful than the person with a good moral record.
"And certainly," he says, "they are more likely to be
nearer to the Kingdom of Heaven, for the very good rea-

son that they are under greater compulsion to be aware of their need."

Bishop Fulton J. Sheen has noted that modern psychology traces man's emotional problems to anxiety. But he contends that the anxiety of contemporary man is different from that of his ancestors on two scores. "In other days men were anxious about their souls, but modern anxiety is principally concerned with the body," he says. "The major worries of today are economic security, health, the complexion, wealth, social prestige and sex.

"The second characteristic of modern anxiety is that it is not a fear of objective, natural dangers, such as lightning, beasts or famine," he observes. "It is subjective, a vague fear of what one believes would be dangerous if it happened. That is why it is so difficult to deal with people who have today's types of anxieties. It does no good to tell them that there is no outside danger, because the danger they fear is inside them and therefore is abnormally real to them."

Any alcoholic can testify to the sagacity of Bishop Sheen's observation that modern man has lost his sense of unity and has become a bundle of nerves. "He is so dissociated, so alienated from himself that he sees himself less as a personality than as a battlefield where a civil war rages between a thousand and one conflicting loyalties," he writes. ". . . He may be likened to a radio that is tuned in to several stations; instead of getting any one clearly, it receives only an annoying static."

Coupled with man's self-estrangement and isolation is his fear of death. He still retains some vision of his lost immortality because, unlike the animal, he is able to contemplate and transcend his own death. "And we also fear it because we have made so poor a use of our years of life," says Bishop Sheen. "When the sense of sin is keen, this fear of facing our own failures may become paradoxically acute, so that the individual wants to lose himself in order not to have to live with himself. This is suicide and nihilism."

It is also a perfect description of the mind of the alcoholic.

But, thank God, the story doesn't have to end there. Both psychology and theology recognize that man needs a new beginning. Freud spoke of "personality reconstruction" and offered a secular salvation with the ringing cry: "Where *id* was, there let *ego* be!"

There is no doubt that a lot of Christians could benefit from therapy under the right therapist. But that is putting the cart before the horse. Alienated man needs to get down on his knees before he gets down on the couch. Salvation is initiated with the simple prayer: "God be merciful to me a sinner" (Luke 18: 13).

Jesus showed the woman taken in adultery that God was the God of the second chance. He is willing to forgive His erring and wayward children seventy-times-seven; but He expects us to demonstrate this same spirit of forgiveness to others (Matthew 18: 22). So great is His compassion and understanding of our human foibles that the psalmist was moved to write: "If thou, O Lord, shouldst mark iniquities, Lord, who could stand? . . . O Israel, hope in the Lord! For with the Lord there is steadfast love, and with him is plenteous redemption" (Psalm 130: 3, 7 RSV).

This does not mean that divine grace comes cheap. For God's love is tempered by His sense of justice. God hates sin even while He loves the sinner. Therefore, He Himself took the crucial step to break the power of sin over captive mankind and restore it to its lost fellowship with Him. Paul put it like this: "For God has done what the law, weakened by the flesh, could not do: sending his own Son in the likeness of sinful flesh and for sin, he condemned sin in the flesh, in order that the just requirement of the law might be fulfilled in us, who walk not according to the flesh but according to the Spirit" (Romans 8: 3, 4 RSV). That is what the Crucifixion of our blessed Lord is all about. He paid the price of your sin and mine. He died in our place.

He breaks the power of canceled sin,
    He sets the prisoner free;
His blood can make the foulest clean;
    His blood availed for me.

But Jesus also confronted that adulterous woman with a challenge that was marked by a warning *and* a promise. "Go," He said, "and sin no more." Couched in those words was the ominous thought that maybe she would not be as fortunate the next time. This does not mean that God is vindictive; it rather suggests that the penalty for sin is built right into the constitution of man. "Know ye not," asks Paul, "that to whom ye yield yourselves servants to obey, his servants ye are to whom ye obey; whether of sin unto death, or of obedience unto righteousness?" (Romans 6: 16).

Alcoholics are just deceiving themselves when they blame God—along with everyone else—for the tragic situation in which they find themselves. For there are some things that even God cannot do. He cannot make a lie the truth; nor can He make a part the whole. And He certainly cannot make a sober man out of the guy who still wants to drink! "No man can serve two masters," declared Jesus. "For either he will hate the one, and love the other; or else he will hold to the one, and despise the other" (Matthew 6: 24).

To the alcoholic who still suffers, the Master says firmly and finally: You cannot serve God and the bottle. One of them has got to go!

But there is a note of promise also couched in that challenge to the adulterous woman. "Go," says Jesus, "and sin no more." That command meant that the most vicious enslavement *can* be broken when a man or a woman *completely surrenders* his or her will to God. The good news of the Gospel proclaims that every sinner can become a saint!

"Jesus was always intensely interested, not only in what a person had been, but also in what a person could be," says William Barclay. "He did not say that what they had done did not matter; broken laws and broken hearts always matter. But Jesus was sure that every man has a future as well as a past."

That is why A.A. speaks of the Twenty-Four Hour Program. None of us can do anything about yesterday; nor can we be sure of the shape of tomorrow. All God expects of any of us is to submit our lives and wills to His fatherly care today. "Therefore do not be anxious about tomorrow," says Jesus. "For tomorrow will be anxious for itself. Let the day's own trouble be sufficient for the day" (Matthew 6: 34 RSV).

Life will not allow us to live on past laurels nor live forever on Cloud Nine. Good sobriety demands that we take a daily moral inventory of our character defects and shortcomings—and then, with God's help, seek to remove them. It also means that we develop the grace to make amends to those whom we have hurt by word and by action. For we cannot expect God's forgiveness to become real in our own lives if we still harbor guilt in our relationships to other people. Jesus put it like this: "If thou bring thy gift to the altar, and there rememberest that thy brother hath ought against thee; Leave there thy gift before the altar, and go thy way; first be reconciled to thy brother, and then come and offer thy gift" (Matthew 5: 23, 24).

Finally, good sobriety is maintained only by giving it away. It is only as we carry the message to the alcoholic who still suffers that our own gratitude develops for the new life we have received by the grace of God. "He that findeth his life shall lose it," Jesus declared. "And he that loseth his life for my sake shall find it" (Matthew 10: 39).

These time-tested principles lie at the very heart of A.A.'s twelve suggested steps for recovery. They are powerful medicine not only for the alcoholic but for anyone whose life is void of meaning, purpose, and a sense of destiny. They also represent the highest goals of the Gospel and modern psychology.

For those who still gag on "this God business," there is one final lesson to be learned from the story of Jesus' encounter with the woman taken in adultery.

Scholars have debated endlessly about the words which our Lord wrote in the sand. How like man to quarrel about the fine points of theology when a human being is rushing headlong into insanity or death. And how like God to use the most obvious things in life—sand, or water, or the humble sparrow—to put the pieces together again.

It has been said that a well-known American communist abandoned Marx to embrace Christ when he was moved to awe and wonder by the sight of his baby daughter's ear.

If some fellow Christians think all of this smacks of too much "natural religion," I can only say that I could take pride in my theology even as I asked for another drink. I was told in seminary all about the *Deus absconditus;* and by the time I finally "hit bottom," I was sure that the *Deus* had absconded from me!

God uses those simple things in life through which His Spirit draws men to His Word. He can make His imprint upon the sand, in a child's ear, or even in a die casting. With me, God took that which I had intellectually accepted and made it experientially real within the fellowship of Alcoholics Anonymous. Gone is that deep anxiety regarding man's purpose and destiny of which Bishop Sheen speaks. And now I can say with Paul through personal experience: "If any man be in Christ, he is a new creature: old things are passed away; behold, all things are become new" (II Corinthians 5: 17).

If God can make a new man out of an egocentric, drunken preacher, something tells me He can also make a new person out of any other alcoholic who is willing to try to stay away from one little drink one day at a time.

God has given us Alcoholics Anonymous to help. But you must open its doors.

CREDITS

1. Reprinted with permission of A.A. World Service, Inc., copyright owner, P.O. Box 459, Grand Central Station, New York, New York 10017

2. "Alcoholism" (Harmondsworth, 1965). Reprinted by permission.

3. "Understanding and Counseling the Alcoholic," Howard J. Clinebell, Jr., Abingdon Press, Nashville, Tennessee.

4. "Gestalt Therapy," Frederick Perls, M.D., Ph.D., Ralph F. Hefferline, Ph.D., and Paul Goodman, Ph.D., New York; The Julian Press, 1951; Delta Paperback, 1964.

CAN YOU BEAT THE RAP?

Check yourself on these self-scoring test
of Risk of Addictive Problems

PART ONE

	YES	NO
Check each statement "yes" or "no."		
1. I have a strong and clear faith in life	___	___
2. Many times I feel uneasy or blue	___	___
3. My home life is as happy as it should be	___	___
4. Some days I feel I am not my real self	___	___
5. I feel sorry for myself and frequently indulge in self-pity	___	___
6. I am moderate in my habits	___	___
7. I often feel guilty or apologetic without knowing why	___	___
8. I am pretty much like everyone else I know	___	___
9. Sometimes I go out of my way to avoid people I dislike	___	___
10. It seems to me I'm going nowhere in my life	___	___
11. I feel there is a barrier between me and the world	___	___
12. My interest or enthusiasm fades quickly	___	___
13. I keep thinking about things I fear	___	___
14. I'm inclined to be serene and relaxed	___	___
15. I feel all alone in the world	___	___
16. My moods change rapidly	___	___

PART TWO

1. Discussions about my drinking (or drug use) make me nervous ⎯⎯ ⎯⎯

2. I am a shaky, jittery person ⎯⎯ ⎯⎯

3. I have had trouble remembering what I did while drinking ⎯⎯ ⎯⎯

4. My drinking (or drug use) has caused me legal, family, health, job or social problems ⎯⎯ ⎯⎯

5. I consume more alcohol (or drugs) than most of my friends do ⎯⎯ ⎯⎯

6. I have sensations of numbness or tingling in my fingers or toes ⎯⎯ ⎯⎯

7. I often want more drinks after the party is over ⎯⎯ ⎯⎯

8. I feel guilty about my drinking (or drug use) ⎯⎯ ⎯⎯

The RAP Scale is based on a 72-question test constructed by a California research psychologist (Manson Evaluation, Quarterly Journal of Studies on Alcohol, Vol. 9, pp. 175-206, Sept. 1948) from frequently heard statements of alcoholics. It is used here by permission of the Monterey Peninsula Council on Alcoholism.

See next page for how to score the test.

How to Score the RAP Test

The answers given here are considered "risk" answers. Total the only answers which coincide with these risk answers. Total Part One and Part Two separately.

Part One
1. No
2. Yes
3. No
4. Yes
5. Yes
6. No
7. Yes
8. No
9. Yes
10. Yes
11. Yes
12. Yes
13. Yes
14. No
15. Yes
16. Yes

Part Two
1. Yes
2. Yes
3. Yes
4. Yes
5. Yes
6. Yes
7. Yes
8. Yes

PART ONE	0 1 2 3 4	5 6 7 8 9	10 11 12 13 14 15 16
	Low	Medium	High

PART TWO	0	1 2	3 4 5 6 7 8
	Low	Medium	High

INTERPRETATION OF YOUR SCORE

LOW on Part One and LOW on Part Two:
You don't have to worry. You are in no danger of addictive problems as long as you continue as you are. If your life situation changes or if you begin to consume more, you will want to check yourself again.

MEDIUM on Part One, LOW on Part Two:
If you are a drinker, probably you will be able to enjoy your drinking all your life without problems. You show no signs whatsoever of any problem. But since you have given "risk" answers to some of the questions, it would be wise to examine yourself in relation to those particular statements. The willingness to develop greater maturity in these areas is good insurance. If you have made as many

188

as six or seven "risk" answers, the caution light is signaling on your use of alcohol and other drugs.

LOW on Part One and MEDIUM on Part Two:
Overdrinking could be a real danger for you. Because you are strong, you are probably confident that you will never have trouble controlling alcohol, that it will never damage your life. But alcohol could boss you, believe it or not. Moderation is your best insurance. If you can't enjoy moderation, there may be a physical reason. If uncomfortable without the usual amount, seek medical advice. Then, if your doctor or your own judgment recommends abstinence, it is good to know that your kind of person can carry out such a decision with comparative ease.

MEDIUM on Part One, MEDIUM on Part Two:
The tendency to overdrink is best counteracted by developing maturity and stability in one's life. The prealcoholic sometimes finds himself using alcohol for comfort or to feel better. If the discomfort, shyness, or unhappiness is great, the person may drink more than he intended and feel worse as a result. If he continues to have this experience he can become a compulsive user of alcohol or drugs, with progressive damage. You can and should learn to enjoy moderation.

HIGH on Part One and LOW on Part Two:
You may be susceptible to alcoholism if you drink. The higher your score in Part One, the more important it is for you to abstain. Wise for you to get active and stay active in a therapy group. Take advantage of the many sources of help in your community. It will be a losing battle for you to try to handle your problems and feelings alone, but with help you can have a much more satisfying life.

LOW on Part One, HIGH on Part Two:
Your answers on Part One indicate a reasonably strong and stable person, but your answers on Part Two indicate progressive dependence on alcohol or drugs. This dependence could be in your case more physiological than psychological. But psychological damage could develop as time goes on **unless you abstain.** (Probably moderation is

not possible for you, especially if you have as many as five risk answers in Part Two.)

HIGH on Part One, MEDIUM on Part Two:
This score indicates high susceptibility to problems with alcohol or drugs, even though you are not yet having obvious trouble. You would be wiser not to drink, at least not until you straighten out the difficulties which your answers to Part One now indicate. Drinking or drugs definitely can make your problems worse, but if you learn to live entirely without these chemical aids you will develop strength and stability which will make your whole life more satisfactory.

MEDIUM on Part One and HIGH on Part Two:
It is quite possible you already recognize that drinking could be a problem for you. You may have had problems as a result of drinking already. If you haven't, don't press your luck. You can't learn to enjoy moderation; better quit now.

HIGH on Part One and HIGH on Part Two:
Alcohol for you is a dangerous drag on physical and emotional health. Your answers show that most of your difficulties are related directly to dependence on alcohol, pills or other drugs. Every department of your life will be better when you break that dependence. And you can. Medical help and continuing therapy is available. The decision to get it is yours. You can still beat the Rap!

Definitions used (In general these are applicable also to the drug user): **Alcoholic** is anyone whose drinking is causing a recurring problem in any department of his life, indicating particularly the onset of loss of control over intake or inability to function adequately. **Prealcoholic** is anyone who is placing undue importance on drinking or having recurring episodes of excessive or inappropriate use (See warning signals). **Nonalcoholic** is a drinker whose use of alcohol is generally moderate, showing no signs of dependence or problems. **Recovered alcoholic** is former problem drinker now abstaining and functioning adequately. (Note: former problem drinkers are rarely able to control intake if they return to drinking.)

REACH OUT
with additional copies of this book...

Simply ask for them at your local bookstore—or order from the David C. Cook Publishing Co., Elgin, IL 60120 (in Canada: Weston, Ont. M9L 1T4).